Telling Y
Data Story

Data Storytelling
for Data Management

Scott Taylor

The Data Whisperer

Technics Publications

Published by:

2 Lindsley Road, Basking Ridge, NJ 07920 USA
https://www.TechnicsPub.com

Edited by Sadie Hoberman
Cover design by Lorena Molinari
Cover Photo by Edwin van Wijk, courtesy of Stibo Systems

First Printing 2020
Copyright © 2020 by Scott Taylor

ISBN, print ed.	9781634628952
ISBN, Kindle ed.	9781634628969
ISBN, ePub ed.	9781634628976
ISBN, PDF ed.	9781634628983

Library of Congress Control Number: 2020946543

To Marianne
The Data Whisperer whisperer

Contents

Acknowledgments

I want to thank all the people who have ever shared their data stories with me. Great stories, exciting, wonderful stories. Stories of pain, struggle, and triumph. From frustrated to exhilarated, from amazing to ridiculous, but always about what data can or should or would do when managed well.

I offer my immense gratitude to my close confidants Marianne Frasco and Jonathan James Cramer, who helped and encouraged me to write this book. They were patient but insistent that I put all these thoughts down. Extra special thanks to my sister Julie Taylor and son Liam Taylor, who fixed my grammar, punctuation, and other sins against language while allowing my voice to come through. All of them constantly challenged my logic and perspective to make it as clear as possible.

I must also thank my parents, who have lovingly encouraged me in everything I have ever done. My mother, Nina, is a shining example of style and creativity. She has an uncanny talent to write in rhyming couplets. My father, Jerry, is a persuasion powerhouse who exudes confidence and gravitas. His advice on writing was the opposite of his advice on making beds: "Start with the easiest part first." And he taught me so much about life and business by beating me to a pulp in Monopoly. Great storytellers both, who use humor, passion, and intelligence to make their points.

I also want to thank all the data management leaders throughout my career who have said to me, "Sure, that sounds good, Scott, but that isn't how it works." I admit to having a talent to spin a tale. But I don't want to only sound good—I want to be accurate as well. I am appreciative of anyone who held me accountable and taught me the importance of technical reality. I treasure those teaching moments and always seek them out.

Thank you, love you always, thank you.

Foreword

My first encounter with Scott Taylor came with high expectations and great anticipation. In 2016, a mutual colleague invited me to a Master Data Management conference in Manhattan, in which Scott would be one of the speakers. This colleague highly recommended that I attend Scott's presentation and raved about his knowledge and experience in the industry.

The conference stretched over a few days and featured a wide range of expert speakers, some on the technical side, others even more technical, and yet others that seemed to speak some completely mythical tech-speak language that I couldn't understand.

And then Scott stepped up to the stage. It was as if the lights dimmed, the crowd hushed, and the clocks stopped. He opened his mouth, and from beginning to the end of his hour in the spotlight, he owned the room, captivating his audience with a flair, a style, and a rich buffet of innovative content that stood out as completely different from all the other presentations. In fact, he didn't really give a presentation at all. He told stories.

His stories had characters. They took place in distinct settings. They were business stories. But, like a seasoned novelist or a trendy screenwriter, he excelled at creating tension by exposing conflict. He laid out common business problems that every member of the audience could relate to, whether they had a technical or a non-technical background. He built alignment with his audience and disarmed them with humor. He entertained while he informed. And we in the audience didn't even realize the extent to which he influenced and evangelized his message, blinded by the sheer enjoyment of hearing him speak.

By the time he delivered the payoff to his story, he had us nodding our heads and wanting to hear more.

After his address, our mutual colleague introduced us in person, and we hit it off immediately. He had a background selling enterprise data management solutions to Fortune 100 and 500 organizations and consulting with clients of all sizes and in all different industries to raise their understanding, awareness, and strategic emphasis on proper data ownership and management.

I've worked at Fortune 100 and 500 organizations such as Pitney Bowes, General Electric, United Health Group, and Morgan Stanley, as well as in mid-market organizations such as Getty Images, Neopost, and AppNexus. I've served in sales operations, marketing, and business innovation roles. Having led global implementations of major enterprise process and technology transformations, I've always understood the importance of having a strong data management program focused on the strategic value of data as a corporate asset.

With my responsibility for implementing the solutions that Scott sold, we both saw the value of influencing corporate executives to apply the necessary resources and investments into ensuring well-documented data policies, clearly-defined roles and responsibilities, business data ownership and data stewardship, well-controlled categorization, access, and visualization and a rigorous, holistic data hygiene program focused on cleanliness, completeness, quality, and compliance.

Like many of Scott's followers, I've spent a career battling the business challenges that he dissects in his storytelling. It's nearly impossible to succeed as a business transformation leader without the level of focus and attention to quality data ownership, mastery, and management that Scott has spent his career discussing with whomever he can get to listen. His simple, but effective message about how to focus on data as a strategic business asset drives growth, efficiency, effectiveness, and customer success, appeals to any business leader, in any functional area at any level of management, and with any amount of technical acumen.

His unique and insightful concepts such as his 4Cs of data structure: Code, Company Category and Country or the 8 'Ates of data usage—including Relate, Validate, Integrate,

Circulate, Aggregate, Communicate, Evaluate and Interoperate, serve as common-sense frameworks for corporate practitioners, like me, to apply in our business environments. His views on the importance of the Chief Data Officer and the distinction between analytics and data management provide valuable food for thought within any corporate culture. Any of Scott's memorable content can be used to influence executive decision-makers to invest in data management programs, platforms, consulting, and talent.

I feel a kinship to Scott in that we both recognize the importance of storytelling as a means for influencing people in a creative, memorable, and influential manner. Outside of my business career, I write, edit, and produce full-length commercial novels. To date, I've published five successful political thrillers, two romantic comedies, and a personal memoir.

A good story needs vibrant characters, a relatable setting, a tense conflict, and a satisfying plot resolution. If you've ever seen Scott's iconic data management videos or his "puppet service announcements," you know about the IT Bee, who speaks in industry-inspired buzzwords, the C "D" O (Chief *Dog* Officer), who refuses to own the data, the Business Monkey, who manages all the monkey business and his wild cast of allegorical characters that he uses to tell his stories. You may have caught any of his many live and virtual presentations in which he's featured experts across the industry telling their data stories. You may well know the horror stories he tells of bad data management practices. And you've inevitably benefited from the resolution in terms of his insights, solution ideas, and best practices he offers in his many channels of communication to his sizeable and rapidly growing global audience. His podcasts and video presentations attract viewers from all over the United States, including multiple countries such as the U.K., Germany, Sweden, Australia, South Africa, Russia, and virtually all corners of the world.

Scott's simple, straightforward, insightful, and innovative storytelling approach comes stuffed with business insight, inspiration, and nuggets of brilliance, wrapped around a narrative style that informs, enlightens, and entertains. Not lost in his off-beat, humorous approach to conveying his wisdom are a wide array of valuable business concepts, ideas, frameworks, and best practices that can assist any business professional in delivering overwhelming benefit to their organization.

- Greg McLaughlin, *Author of fictional novels and Executive Director, Transformation & Technology Innovation at Morgan Stanley*

Every Enterprise has a Data Story to Tell

Good decisions made on bad data

Are just bad decisions

You don't know about...yet.

Everything we do today turns to data. As your business and business processes go from analog to digital, everything you do turns to data. Yet, enterprises of all sizes are struggling to make sense of it all. Instead of delivering incredible value, much of this data is creating a lot of chaos. Finding value in data is elusive and frustrating. How do you determine the truth and derive meaning from all that data to grow, improve, and protect your business?

What is your business case for data? I suggest *it is the very business you are in.* I assume your business purpose is to **deliver value to your relationships through your brands** *at scale.* Delivering value to relationships through brands has always been at the core of business. To do it *at scale*

9

takes technology. Technology requires data. Data requires data management.

When you try to determine the truth and derive meaning from data, where do you begin? I begin with the simplest, most important data of all. It is the data about your *relationships* and your *brands*. Your relationships: customer, vendor, partner, prospect, supplier, citizen, patient, client, or consumer.

How reliable is your data about those relationships? Duplicates? Confusing hierarchies? Missing classifications and segments? Conflicting geographies and markets? What about the data on your brands? Products, services, offerings, SKUs, banners, locations, materials, ingredients, and concepts? That might be a bit of a mess too.

Data management is one of the most important, and overlooked, competencies at most enterprises. It is an unsung hero behind many business initiatives. If you already know that, then this book will help you explain it to others. If you don't realize that, then this book will help you understand.

The entire purpose of this book is to help secure stakeholder involvement and executive commitment to managing data—to help you fund and support data management as a systematic, consistent, and fundamental part of your business. Not a project, but a program, Not a tactical exercise, but a strategic imperative.

If you are like most companies, you have multiple systems and workflows that support separate departments and divisions. Your relationship and brand data get created with differing definitions that lack internal standards.

You may already know how to fix your data, but your business leaders ignore your advice. Your business has no interest in your beautiful data "quality" dashboards. Your stakeholders don't care about data "hygiene." When presenting endlessly on your data maturity assessment, you start to sound adolescent. You fail to gain a commitment to support your data management efforts.

To better leverage the value of data management across an enterprise, the essentials must first be understood. This book covers the strategic and foundational benefits of data management, including industry trends, basic definitions, business-oriented frameworks, and identifying obstacles to help you tell your data story.

When you explain it to the business, they are nodding "yes" on the outside and nodding off on the inside. This book is about why foundational data is important for your organization, and most of all, it is about how to *talk* about it. I am an expert in ways to talk about the value of data management. To win your leaders over, you need to tell a better story.

I want to help you with that story. I call it your *Data Story*. You probably already know it—you just need some help telling it. Let me offer you some new ways to talk about what you already know. Since this is a book about telling data stories, I will share it through stories divided into sections:

- **My data story**. Why I know what I know and why you should listen to me.

- **The current state of data management storytelling.** The two kinds of data stories and why you need both.

- **Everyone's data story**. A collection of classic, foundational data situations relevant to all enterprises.

- **Framing your data story**. A set of simple frameworks to help articulate data value.

- **Selling your data story**. Tips on creating a compelling narrative.

- **Building your data story**. Aligning your data management efforts with the strategic intentions of your enterprise.

- **Finding the data story**. Examples of enterprise scenarios that require data management.

I have traveled the world talking to people about how *they* talk about their data. In conference rooms, boardrooms, at events, on panels, in person, on stage, on the phone, or via webcam, I have engaged with thousands of people, at hundreds of companies, in every vertical, at every stage of maturity. I have found patterns and motifs and universal themes. I have distilled them in this book. When it sounds and feels familiar, it should bring you relief that you are not alone.

This slim volume is designed to be given to your leadership and business stakeholders. You will probably agree with most of what I write and recognize the direct applications to your business. So, give this to them to help explain what you are after. The people in your organization who have no time to understand the technical complexity but have all the money to fund your programs. The people you need to help you manage and own your data. You want them to quickly go through the transition from "I have no idea what you are talking about" to "How can we survive without this?" Because as we all know, data can be the difference between surviving and thriving.

I want to share tactical examples and best practices to get your data management story created and accepted by the business. I sit in the middle as a translator and storyteller. We all have a role to play, and that is mine. I want to help you get more funding and support for an area that becomes more mission-critical with every new advancement in technology. The need for data management is everywhere across your company. It is *macro-trend agnostic* yet often hidden in plain sight.

This book is to help you discover that data story. It is already there in your organization. Every enterprise is already working with data.

As everything you do turns to data, this is your opportunity to make the most of it. There is plenty of complexity in the data space. Yet it is filled with simple truths. I want to help you simplify the complex. Let's work together to make sure your enterprise data management story ends happily ever after.

CHAPTER 1

My Data Story

Why I know what I know and why you should listen to me

I am Scott Taylor—The Data Whisperer. I help calm data down. That's what we all do in data management. We help calm data down. Data can be unruly. Data can be messy. Data can be dirty. Data can be corrupt. Data can be Big.

Data can be unstructured. Data is often a mess! To get the value we need out of data, we all need to calm it down.

I also help calm *people* down when they think about data. Some people, especially business leaders, can be confused. People can be anxious, annoyed, and befuddled when it comes to data. Once people can think about data calmly, they can focus on understanding the value.

> **Spoiler Alert**: Although I am *The Data Whisperer*, I don't do much *whispering*. If you have ever heard me speak, seen me present, watched my videos, or listened to a podcast interview, you know I can get downright loud. I am passionate about the strategic value of proper data management.

I focus on the strategic WHY rather than the technical HOW, the tactical WHAT, or the organizational WHO. All of these aspects are important. But business leaders must understand the WHY before investing in the HOW, WHAT, and WHO.

I will confess right up front—I am not a hands-on data practitioner. I have never worked in data management at an enterprise. I have never created analytics or even managed enterprise data directly. You may wonder how I know what I know. Why should you listen to me?

I have over 25 years of experience in the master data, reference data, metadata, MDM (master data management), data governance space, and I spent those decades solving data management challenges for large global enterprises. I also helped data content owners and innovative tech brands tell their data stories. I have enlightened countless business executives on the value of proper data management by stressing strategic rationale and business alignment rather than technical implementation and system integration. I sold data management services in the form of structured data content for my entire career.

Figure 1 I love MDM wherever I can find it, so I took this selfie in front of Michaelson Door Manufacturing

Along my journey, I have spoken to thousands of data and business professionals from every part of an organization. I have heard many versions of the same underlying data story. Like the Ancient Greek epics and Shakespeare's classics, data management has stories of heroics and love, loss and survival, journey and struggle, dreams, and aspirations. Stories of pain, of frustration, of exhilaration, of triumph. Stories of business transformation based on better data management. I saw first-hand what others could do with data and eventually discovered the similarities of these experiences.

I always loved the taxonomy side, the structural side, the ontology side of data. I think I may be hardwired for this space because my parents told me when I was a child, instead of building with my Lego blocks, I sorted them. If your kids sort their Lego blocks, they are good candidates to be in the data business. Encourage them.

People often talk about being disruptive. We all want to be disruptive in technology. I come by that honestly as well. My fourth-grade teacher wrote in my report card: "Scott is disruptive…and distracting to others." I take that as a compliment. We all need to be disruptive in a positive way.

In a variety of strategic marketing, GTM, innovation, and consulting roles, I worked with some of the world's most iconic business data brands, including Dun & Bradstreet, Nielsen, Microsoft, and WPP/Kantar.

You can only be successful in data sales and marketing if you have useful data and explain how to use it. The number one reason clients don't renew a data license is that they didn't use the data—not because it was bad—so if they don't put the data to work, they never see the value.

I sold and marketed data management services in the form of structured data. Even more specifically, I didn't *sell* data. I sold licenses to data. Data itself is rarely sold. Successful data providers sell a license to their data, which allows a user to access it for a predetermined period under specific right-to-use guidelines. The user can only rent the content. In the data business, possession is *no tenths of the law*.

I thrive in the gap between technical practitioners and business leadership: those who know HOW to do it and those who want to understand WHY. I have always worked in syndicated data. That is my favorite kind. I believe it is the most valuable. Syndicated data providers create a data set to serve as a baseline for an entire market or vertical or type of company. That is hard.

They need standards and definitions and taxonomies and all the other structural things that make data resilient and trustworthy so an entire market can agree on the same point of view. Once they set that standard, this data often becomes a "currency" or "Lingua Franca of a market."

I knew nothing about data when I got my first job in the data business in 1994. I worked for a small group called *Trade Dimensions*, which was part of VNU, a global publishing and information services company that eventually evolved into what is now known as Nielsen. We had a retail location data product we called "a book of stores," delivered as an *electronic database*. I guess *electronic* made it sound cool. At least it did in 1994. Sometimes we had to give clients a separate computer because our 30,000-record database was too big for them to manage. That much data would fit on the smallest thumb drive you get free at a convention today, and you'd still have plenty of room.

This database of retail store locations was of interest to consumer packaged goods (CPG) manufacturers in the United States. Any company that made something you might find in a supermarket would need this data. I began to realize that our clients were doing unique things with our content. They were finding new ways to use this highly-structured data to unduplicate their records, add hierarchy, leverage classification schemes, and standardize geographies. Simple yet powerful applications. The sorts of use cases that require master data. But this was before MDM (master data management) was an established category of commercial software. It became apparent to me that this was more than a tactical list of stores. More strategically positioned, it was a master file of customer locations. Long before we knew what to call it, we provided *master data as-a-service*. I didn't come up with the term M-DaaS for another 20 years.

Get Linked!

Introducing TDLINX
The Trade Dimensions set of universal codes for the retail world. We have a code for every store. And every chain, buying office and supplier. Plus our codes are already widely established and accepted as the de facto industry standard.

Don't Guess, Know!
If you use the codes, you and the companies that serve you can spend more time working and less time guessing.

Get the Inside Advantage
Communicating easily and seamlessly to outside companies is just one advantage of **TD**LINX. Every company also has its own customer files (field sales lists, ship-to's, bill-to's). **TD**LINX gives you the ability to communicate easily and seamlessly within your own organization, across divisions, departments and systems.

Start Talking the Same Language
Tremendous effciencies are achieved when companies speak the same language. Simply put, a huge number of hours are spent getting identities straight, matching lists again and again. **TD**LINX solves that problem. Any two parties with the Trade Dimensions codes can talk to each other.

Start Reaping Operational Benefits
Let us see what you have and how to link it inside and out.

Get Linked!
Call Scott Taylor at 203 977-7625

TDLINX
The Universal Language of Stores and Accounts
Our codes are in the most popular micromarketing systems; Trade Dimensions clients have them; and these marketing, merchandising and promotional services companies have them:

Merchandising
• DSI
• National MegaForce
• PIA Merchandising
• Retail Support Force
• SPAR Marketing Force
• TDS

Sampling/Demos
• SmartDemo
• Sunflower
• Super Marketing
• US Concepts

In-Store
• Catalina
• Coinstar
• MediaOne
• News America In-Store
• Retail Marketing Network

Figure 2 TDLinx Announcement from 1996.

Clients also used the unique number we had on each record to integrate internal and external data sources, cut across system silos, and communicate seamlessly with their execution partners. In 1996, we branded this identifier as the TDLinx code (TD stood for Trade Dimensions).

The business was a huge success. We established a proprietary standard for store and account locations across the CPG landscape. We built a network of promotional, marketing, merchandising, and service providers who also began working off the same data—or links to the same data. We created a proprietary yet straightforward data language for use in a very complicated industry. It became a defacto standard for store location identification. We saw Coke and Pepsi agree. It was a remarkable experience to witness the delight clients took in our data.

I learned from my clients the profound benefits of common, structured, master data. I quickly recognized what they were doing was applicable in different industries and across other domains. Master data, as the representative output of strategic data management, had applications for every business. I never looked back.

Master Data is often referred to as the nouns of your business: customers, vendors, brands, locations, and so on. If you look in Wikipedia, you will find the definition I put there: Master data is a common source of basic business data used across multiple systems, applications, and processes. *Nice and simple. It has been unchallenged in Wikipedia for ten years. So, please don't touch it.*

Based on the success of TDLinx, I went on to become part of a global innovation group at Nielsen and searched all across the company landscape for master and reference data productization opportunities. They were everywhere. The company couldn't support the operational efforts to create new offerings, but I learned a lot. I became an independent consultant and did the same thing working with some of the most extensive and varied sets of data imaginable. My goal was to find foundational, structured data opportunities.

I worked at Dun & Bradstreet, who was a world leader in master data but, as a brand, didn't know how to articulate it clearly. My job was to create a better story about their master data services. Believe it or not, it took a lot of convincing. Some of their marketing people said, "we don't like the idea you came up with, calling it master data." I told them, "it isn't my idea. That is what you call this type of data. We just need to talk about it the right way." One large master data client of theirs told me, "I know why I am buying it, but they don't know why they are selling it to me." That feedback stuck with me. The fact that D&B now globally markets a vital part of their business as *master data* is the result of my work.

It wasn't always like this. I had many failures. Early on at Nielsen, I met with the chief revenue officer of one of the world's largest bakeries. He stood up from behind his desk, making a goodbye movement, and simply said,

"That all sounds very complicated. I just have a simple problem—I need to figure out how to sell more bread. You have not convinced me that you can help."

He was wrong. What I presented could help him "sell more bread." But I was wrong. I made it too complicated, too technical, and too far removed from his business. It was a long, quiet drive back to the airport after that meeting.

For those who understood it, data management is a fascinating part of the business. At times it can be considered a secret weapon. But many people didn't understand it. And those who did understand had trouble explaining it to the business stakeholders. I was able to articulate the value of this type of data and what it can do for an organization.

Eventually, I felt there was space to bring a new voice to the data management community. There is a certain amount of frustration from people who have been doing this forever but realize, "my company still doesn't understand."

You can find plenty of people who are excited about analytics, but not that many people were excited about data management. I took my skills as a storyteller and a content creator and focused them on building editorial content supporting the strategic value of proper data management.

I honed my ability to give folks who think they are in a unique situation the solace in realizing that the person sitting next to them has the same problems. If you are in manufacturing, financial services, or a digital start-up—all very different businesses with different business models— at the foundational level, you all have the same sort of data problems. Indeed, not identical, but they are more the same than they are different.

I, too, am a firm and fervent believer in the power and importance of proper data management and have spent my career successfully convincing senior business leaders to invest in it. To win over business stakeholders, data management leadership must craft a compelling narrative that builds urgency, reinvigorates enthusiasm, and evangelizes WHY their programs enable the strategic intentions of their enterprise. If the business leaders whose support and engagement you seek do not understand and accept the WHY, they will not care about the HOW.

I am here to help you become a better storyteller. More specifically, to help you recognize and explain the exact ways data will enable your organization to grow, improve, and protect your business.

I could have titled this book, *"Winning with Data Management,"* but no one would have believed me. If you are like many of the thousands of data professionals I have met over my career, you struggle to communicate the value of data to your business stakeholders and senior leadership. That audience doesn't understand you. In some cases, they will not understand the words you use, the pictures you show, or the techniques you have mastered.

The type of story you need to construct is a pitch. You are *selling* the idea of data management. Solving your selling problem, you need to work on what I refer to (with a knowing wink to Big Data) as *The 3Vs of Data Management Storytelling*—Vocabulary, Voice, and Vision. In most cases:

- Your **Vocabulary** is confusing
- Your **Voice** is discordant
- Your **Vision** is blurred

When communicating to executive leadership, skip the technical details, the feature functionality, and the reference architecture, and focus on:

- Establishing an accessible **Vocabulary**
- Harmonizing to a common **Voice**
- Illuminating the business **Vision**

If you are a data leader or practitioner, you are already well-versed in data management, data governance, master data, reference data, metadata, business glossaries, data dictionaries, data catalogs, taxonomies, ontologies, hierarchies, identifiers, classification schemas, and beyond. You may find the advice in this book simplistic. You may think it superficial at times or lacking in technical nuances. That is deliberate. To spread a message, you need to make it simple. Business stakeholders need an accessible way to understand the fundamentals of what makes data important—free of buzz words, technical descriptions, and hyped-up urgency.

You may already understand the programming and technical requirements. How to code, how to architect, how to implement these solutions. If you do, then you know more about that than I do. But what you may learn from me is how to explain the value of those things to your business stakeholders.

You probably need more funding to manage data because it doesn't seem important enough to your board of directors. It is not the cool stuff. It is not the sexy stuff that everybody's talking about. If you want funding, if you want support, if you want stakeholder engagement, you must be able to articulate the *value* of your proposition. That is true for every business proposition, but for Data Leaders, it can be particularly challenging.

As I help you construct your data management story, I focus almost exclusively on the *data* part. Very specifically, on the importance of structured, foundational data like master data, reference data, and metadata. My rationale is that these are tangible outputs of proper enterprise data management. This is where data starts. These help the entire organization. They are indeed the foundational piece-parts of every business. They are a mandatory requirement. But they are rarely understood or even recognized by enterprise leadership and business stakeholders. As an example, my friend and data governance expert, Peter Kapur, advises á la *Fight Club,* "The first rule of talking about metadata to the business is to not talk about metadata to the business."

To me, this all seems remarkably simple and straightforward. I have a career of experience telling data management stories. But most people, on both sides of this storytelling effort, have trouble getting it straight. They are data practitioners and data leaders by trade but lack some of the soft skills needed to communicate to the business effectively. That's why I felt the need to write this book. My intention is to help data management experts learn a more practical approach that helps business leaders understand.

Data and technology are rooted in hard skills: coding, stewardship, governance, architecture, and process design. Storytelling may be contrary to your natural strengths. Articulating the value and getting support often takes soft skills like storytelling. It is useful because it taps into what makes us all human. Data management storytelling is evangelism. You need to get people to *believe* in what you are saying, even if they can not see it. You need them to *practice* what you will preach.

A message to business leaders

I can offer some simple explanations about why data management is essential for your organization. Without going deep into technical concepts and processes that you do not need to understand, I will focus on the importance of the outputs. I will share ways you can think about what foundational data does. If you resist data management because you think your organization can survive without data, then just put this book down. Prepare yourself for failure.

If, however, you realize data is necessary but want to know more about why managing it is so critical, then please read on. My objective is to give you the conversational basics to understand why data management needs to be a strategic imperative in your organization. I want to provide you with some tips on understanding what the heck some of your data practitioners are trying to tell you.

A message to data scientists

As I have become involved in the broader Data Science community, I hear many conversations about programming languages and other technical aspects of the role. But a recurring struggle I recognize from data scientists is regarding their need to get "closer to business." Many of them look for ways to show how their talents can add value to their enterprise. This book is for you as well.

If you are a data scientist, then you need to understand your company's data story. The more you can align your work to the core value your company delivers, the more successful you will be. My objective is to give you a way to understand the essence of your business, and help you learn how to seek out and engage with your business leaders to understand their issues and objectives. If you can turn your talent towards making data a powerful tool for your company's growth, improvement, and protection, then you will be successful.

The stories I don't tell

If you are familiar with the classic database and software design phases of *conceptual, logical,* and *physical*: I am fantastic at conceptual, I can get technically through logical, but I don't get *physical*. I don't touch anything. I leave that to the data engineers, architects, and other practitioners who know how to get those things done. I have great respect for that expertise. I have none of it.

I will not cover the *management* part of data management. You will find very little, if anything, on the other vital topics within data management such as governance, stewardship, security, privacy, modeling, storage, operations, warehousing, design, architecture, and ethics.

Don't come to me if you are looking for help in choosing tools, processes, and programming tips for data integration and data science. This is not a technical book. I have never done any coding. Although I studied KAFKA in school, it was when I read *Metamorphosis*. Panda and Python are animals I visit at the zoo. NoSQL means I shouldn't watch Rocky IV, V, and VI. But I do know that a Pirate's favorite programming language is RRRRRRRRR!!!

Although this book is about the value of data management, I offer no tools or measures for data quality. You should look elsewhere for benchmarks and best practices for measuring and increasing data quality. In terms of positioning data management, I will comment on the value of the word *quality* later on. It isn't pretty.

This book is not about a data organization. I offer no tips on how to organize a data department. I do believe DATA should be its own department in an organization, and certainly separate from IT. It seems to be an organizational flaw that data was under technology. I am pleased that it is becoming, as they say, closer to the business. There are wonderful experts in the market, many of whom I know and admire and have valuable advice: Caroline Carruthers, Peter Jackson, Peter Aiken, Martin Treder, to name a few, have all written books about the role of a Chief Data Officer.

I can't help you with Data Maturity. There are many, probably too many, data maturity models. All the major industry analysts and software platform vendors offer maturity models. Get one and see where you are. George Firican does an excellent job tracking and comparing data maturity models.

I offer no insight into data monetization. As Doug Laney, the father of *INFONOMICS*, reminded me when I shared the subject area of my book with him: "Scott, please leave that topic to the experts." No worries, Doug. If you want to monetize your data, however, you better have robust data management in place. If your data isn't any good, no one will pay you for it. If data is not already your product (and I bristle when people suggest "every company is a data company" because it isn't), then watch out. At its most basic level, the data business is a different kind of business. Most people don't know the first thing about actually being in the data business. Many are tempted by the *last thing,* which is: you *might* make money at it. But read Doug's book *INFONOMICS* for guidance.

I won't help you with the accountabilities, roles, and responsibilities of data governance and stewardship — no practical advice on who does what and where in which part of the organization. If you need that sort of help, I encourage you to look into the work of exceptional consultants whose thinking I admire. Look up Nicola Askham, Lara Gureje, George Firican, Bob Seiner, Frank Cerwin, Anthony Algmin, Irina Steenbeek, Henrik Gabs Liliendahl, and Aaron Zornes, among others.

This book won't help you write a business glossary and data dictionary, create a data catalog, deliver your data models, unify your internal tribal language for entities, or find a way to gain consensus among stakeholders on definitions. You should do all that. They are mandatory for data success. Once your leaders support data management holistically, you can gain the authority to complete those tasks. To get that support, they need to hear your data story first. That is where I can help. They will more easily participate in all of the above once you get them enchanted.

You cannot skip any of those things. But if you do all of those and still can't tell the right story, you continue to risk having data management relegated to the "why do we have to do this again?" topics for upper management. That is the purpose of this book. To help you talk about it better. To help you convey the value, importance, and urgency of the work you already know how to do.

The stories I do tell

Most data management leaders whom I have known and loved are genuinely passionate about the value of data. They understand to their core that data can grow, improve, and protect their businesses. Many have challenges, however, articulating that value in a business-accessible manner—especially when competing for funding with better storytelling peers from sales and marketing.

I look for the essence of things. I spent time boiling concepts down. The data and technology space can get very complicated and confusing very quickly. I like to talk about it in straightforward accessible ways that get people excited about something they didn't realize they should be doing. That's my forte—finding those nuggets, those stories, those examples, those constructs to describe very complicated parts of data.

Many business processes, opportunities, challenges, obstacles, and problems get better with better data. Better data is better. Don't let anyone tell you anything different.

Proving it is the hard part. When you have a minute with your CEO, do you proudly show them your latest reference data architecture? Do you drone on about low data quality? Do you rely on overused confusing metaphors like "data is the new oil?"

Why are those statements important to your business? They aren't really. That approach has become a cliché and will not drive any action. It will not secure funding or deepen engagement.

While data storytelling and data literacy efforts are gaining market traction, these tend to be more focused on using business intelligence and analytics outputs in a business setting or a relationship-building process. Data Storytelling is predominantly telling stories *with* data. A data management narrative, however, focuses on telling stories *about* the data. Data management leaders who seek to improve soft skills and execute simple storytelling techniques will be more likely to gain a rightful place for their initiatives on their organization's strategic plan.

CHAPTER 2

The Current State of the Data Management Story

Data Storytelling and Data Literacy are probably the hottest non-technical trends in the technology-related space. Neither of them directly supports data management. That has to change.

> There are two kinds of Data Storytelling: Stories WITH data (to support the use of analytics) and stories ABOUT data (reinforcing the importance of data management).

Keep in mind that there are two types of data storytelling. The most popular type of *data storytelling* is generally about Analytics. It guides the use of insight to drive business action. Many excellent experts and thought leaders have created content to help analytics and data science professionals. Coupled with data literacy, these efforts go a long way to assist in the effective delivery and use of insights in an enterprise. Industry experts like Kate Strachnyi, Nancy Duarte, Cole Nussbaumer Knaflic, Mico Yuk, Brent Dykes, Jordan Morrow, and Zack Mazzoncini all lead formal practices in how to better communicate with data through graphics, display, visualization, dashboarding and business-building techniques. It is a deep and vital knowledge area of crucial importance to every data-driven organization.

It is time, however, to expand the realm of Data Storytelling to recognize the role of data management. It is the story about why data is vital to an organization and why it needs to be managed strategically. While an analytics data story is storytelling *with* data and using it, the data management story is *about* data and making it. Both are important. They are connected. Segmenting these two data storytelling types helps clarify your focus and purpose. Every organization needs to do both.

When I read Gartner's definition of data literacy—*the ability to read, write, and communicate with data in context*—I don't see anything about data management. The majority of time and focus in the field of Data Storytelling and Data Literacy is spent *explaining analytics.*

For more context, I see two big buckets in the broader data space: data (meaning data management) and analytics (some sort of business intelligence). *Analytics,* and the extended capabilities based on business intelligence, such as artificial intelligence, machine learning, data science, and data visualization, focus on making data more useful for an organization. This is where you derive MEANING. The activities around data management ensure data is trustworthy for an organization: data governance, data quality, data catalogs, business glossaries, master data, reference data, metadata, MDM, RDM, and PIM. This is where you determine the TRUTH.

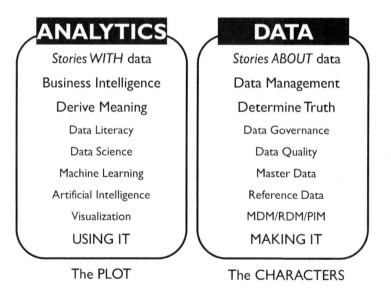

Figure 3 There are two kinds of Data Storytelling.

Data Storytelling is not just about analytics. But if you look at the content published about data storytelling, it is devoted to tips on visualization, dashboards, charts, graphs, and other ways to explain analytics. Analytics can bring all sorts of value to an enterprise as long as the data is trustworthy. Devoid of data management, however, analytics data storytellers have no story to tell— analytics create the *plot*, but the *characters* come from data management. Here's a simple example of an analytics data story headline:

Our market share is down in our top regions, so we need to increase promotional pricing.

Through analytics, this storyteller has proven that market share in certain regions is down and recommends that incentivizing prospects with a new offer will help drive volume and potentially lead to share increases. All the characters in this story come from data management. Calculating *market share* requires a clear definition of categories and competitors. *Sales* is an aggregated form of transactions. Transactions are made up of the intersection of a *customer* record and a *product* record at a given time for a particular price—essentially a *relationship* and a *brand*. Data management governs the definition of customer and product. Standardized market definitions are agreed upon through the work of data management. Yes, the business has input into the definitions, but the story falls apart if those entities are not clearly defined. Questions abound: What do you mean by top regions? Which customers? What products?

Every enterprise has a data story to tell. They must tell it for two particular reasons: First, investment in data management is a crucial component for the success of the business. This investment should be an on-going, strategic initiative, not a one-time ad-hoc project. Most C-Level business executives, company boards, and business stakeholders don't understand that. It is not because they aren't smart or aware—they simply haven't been exposed to the need for data management in a business-accessible way with a strategic perspective. To get their attention, they need to hear a narrative that captures their hearts and minds and convinces them that data management is not an option.

Secondly, the louder, cooler, and in many cases, "sexier" trends fail without proper data management. Many massive investments are woefully underperforming. The value of every digitally transformative customer-facing initiative, every data science and analytics-based project, every as-a-service offering, every foray into e-commerce, and every enterprise software implementation is inextricably linked to the successful output of data management efforts. Although it is a simple function of *garbage in garbage out,* that slogan rarely serves to drive any sustainable executive action.

We need to speak up. How many of you sit silently when a BI thought-leader boasts, "without analytics, data is just a cost center" or "data has no value unless it is made into analysis." That is your work! A baker would never say, "flour is worthless unless I make it into bread," because they have respect for the ingredients. There is no doubt that business intelligence provides incredible capabilities, but without proper data management, those efforts are futile. Challenge the analytics community to end this type of zero-sum portrayal of data vs. analytics value. It doesn't help either group gain executive support.

The need for data management has never been greater. The convergence of social, mobile, cloud, and information patterns are driving new business scenarios within the macro-trend of digital transformation. This transformation unlocks untapped value, innovative experiences, and disruptive business models. In a digitally-transformed organization, data moves seamlessly from workflow to workflow and between external partners. Users can spend their time improving their relationship experience rather than questioning the data.

The road to data management ruin is paved with good intentions, both strategic and tactical. Business Stakeholders, at all levels, may have limited exposure to the critical importance of enterprise data management. Typical data management program failings include, but are not limited to:

- Data management funded as a project instead of a program

- Failure to show immediate value

- Expanding scope with unclear definitions

- Lack of compliance and support from other departments

- Underestimating the cultural mind-shift, organizational support, and change management required for success

- Lack of direct Return on Investment (ROI)

- Unrealistic scope definition—often referred colloquially in retrospect as "boiling the ocean"

- Execution as an IT- and technology-led effort

- Cultural apathy, siloed behavior, skunkworks analytics, and a general disregard for data governance requirements

You defined the use cases, worked on the implementation plan, and provided a clear return on investment. You thought you proved it all. But you did not break through to the people with all the money who have no time to hear you out.

To evangelize data management programs, leaders must create a compelling narrative. In a recently published declaration, *Data Management Has Failed!*, Tom Redman, John Ladley, and a host of other long-time leaders from DAMA, the international data management association, drafted a call-to-action recommending "bold, powerful moves" needed to secure business leader support for data management. They suggest: (1) remove technology from the conversation, (2) focus on outcomes, not minutiae, and (3) earn genuine senior-level engagement. These are indeed worthy actions, but perhaps the real crux of the problem lurks deep in Redman and Ladley's observation that "as a community, we have failed to educate our leaders…and craft messages that people will listen to."

They are correct. There is too much tech talk that makes data management *messaging* very hard to listen to. The current data management sales pitch simply isn't convincing. There are multiple reasons why data management programs may fail, yet an overwhelming majority suffer from an inability to demonstrate and communicate business alignment.

It doesn't help that data management efforts aren't considered exciting, innovative, or "cool." Meanwhile, business intelligence, in all its iterations (artificial intelligence, machine learning, AutoML), enjoys a disproportionate amount of exposure, limelight, and support. The elevation of these practices to near-heroic stature continues to overemphasize business intelligence over data management.

Hot trends give the cold shoulder to data management. Where is the active voice of data management in data storytelling, data literacy, and data visualization? I don't hear it. Data Science, in all its sexiest-profession glamour, glosses over the core value of data management. We seem numb to claims that data scientists spend 60-90% of their time *munging* and *wrangling* data. Those cute terms mask the real issue. Having access to better-managed data will avoid much of that munging and wrangling—data free of duplicates, with a well-governed, expertly-stewarded structure for hierarchies, taxonomies, and geographies.

Additionally, McKinsey Digital identified six data management best practices in their paper *Designing Data Governance That Delivers Value:*

1. **Secure top management's attention**
2. Integrate with primary transformation themes
3. Prioritize data assets and focus data leadership accordingly
4. Apply the right level of governance
5. Choose iterative and focused implementation
6. **Generate excitement for data**

The first and last items support the need for better storytelling. To capture top management's attention and generate excitement for data, you must tell a compelling data story about data management.

The story of foundational data

If you have a problem related to technology, it is usually associated with three things: hardware, software (and I'll include any form of coding in there), and data. Before you start yelling about "people and culture and process," just go with me on this.

Let's say your CEO's quarterly reports aren't correct, or your customer experience is in shambles. Where is the problem? Is it the hardware? Probably not. You have a reliable and secure cloud vendor. Is it the software? Doubtful. Commercial software pretty much does what it is supposed to do. Is it the data? Most likely. And within the data, is it the analytics? Sometimes. But analytics in production is usually well-tested. Where is the problem? The root cause tends to be in the underlying data representing the structure of the output: master data, reference data, metadata—all in the scope of data management. If your customer hierarchy is wrong, your reports are untrustworthy, and your Customer Experience is a mess. If there is a data breach, odds are someone, somehow, falsified their identity. Authenticated identity is a crucial benefit of highly-structured data.

When your data is good, it is very, very good, and when it is bad, it is horrid.

The classic disruptors in every industry, Airbnb, Uber, Amazon, for example, all thrive on well-managed data. Their services fail without the master, reference, and metadata that fuels them. When you tap your thumb on the phone, a car arrives. When you search for a product, you may be served with new alternatives. It isn't magic. Of course, it takes systems, but without the foundational data, it will not work.

How do you start to articulate the value of this kind of data? Here are a few ideas:

- It is a *common language* for your organization. A common language for common definitions for the most important relationships of your business: customers, vendors, partners, prospects, and your brands, products, assets, and services.

- It is about *rows and columns*. If you think about a nifty data visualization technique, let's call it a "table" or a basic chart. People are good at columns, but they are not good at rows. That is the master data part—all those rows. The data that makes up the rows is what the data in the columns is about. Adding columns is easy—aligning rows is hard.

- It is about *truth and meaning*. It isn't chicken or egg here. It is egg and omelet. Data is the primary ingredient for analytics. You have to determine the truth in your data before you can derive any meaning from analytics.

- It is about *caring for your relationships*. How do you grow and improve and protect your business? And I know there are some other things that people do in their business, but if you think about it—growing, improving, and protecting your business—that is most of what you do. Structured data can help you do all three at the same time.

- It is about *making good decisions*. That's all businesspeople want to do is make good decisions. *But good decisions made on bad data are just bad decisions you don't know about…yet.*

Your data story is about your data pain

Data management can equal pain. I have been in this business long enough to notice people do not use cute little business euphemisms like "we have a challenge" or "we have a hurdle." They talk about *physical pain*. I learned this early in my career when I was selling to a sales organization, and the head of sales said, "You know Scott, we can slice and dice our data any way we want to. All I have to do is push a button?" Then this courageous sales analyst at the end of the table stood up and said, "Sir, I'm the button." You are probably "the button" in your organization. That hurts.

I'm going to share an example of pain. Be prepared. I call it naked data. There's no way to hide from it:

The New York Times Media Group	NESTL	7 11
The New York Times Company	NESTL F	7 - 11
New York Times Co.	NESTL F	7.11
New York Times, The	NESTL L	7/11
The N.Y. Times	Nestle	7\11
New York Times	NESTLE	7=11
N.Y. Times	NESTLÉ	7-11
NY Times	NESTLE'	
NYTimes	NESTLE-	SEVEN ELEVEN
Nytimes	NESTLE/	SEVEN/ELEVEN
	NestlΘ	SEVEN-ELEVEN
	NestlΘ-	
	NESTRAD	

Figure 4 Separate processes produce duplicate records with inconsistent naming conventions.

That's the problem. These examples are from embarrassingly large global enterprises who don't know what they are doing with the *New York Times*, can't figure out a way to consistently input Nestlé, don't know how to report on 7-Eleven. And this last column here came from a manufacturer that put people into stores. They had a retail location file with over 275 different configurations of the 7-Eleven Banner name—lots of creativity in the field, none of it selling products. If you think the software is always going to solve the problem, you put this in Excel, and you get July 11th (except for those of you from the EU who get November 7th.)

Figure 5 Example of the lack of data governance. The software doesn't always fix it.

Find or create an example like this from your own organization's data. Although I am always talking about the high-level conceptual, strategic approach, anchoring it with examples of physical reality has a potent effect. You cannot talk your way out of this sort of bad data. Malcolm Hawker of Gartner calls it *the shame report*. "Sometimes you need to rub people's nose in their bad data," he says. Put that in front of your business stakeholders who don't understand why you can't get the right kind of analytics. It works because it hurts.

The Golden Rule of Data

GIGO—*Garbage In, Garbage Out.* Some know this as *rubbish in, rubbish out.* Every data professional learns this on their first day. It is an inescapable reality, as inevitable as Newtonian physics. What goes up must come down. What goes in must come out. This has become a standard answer. It is almost a throwaway comment mumbled by a senior analyst in the back of the room.

"Why are these reports wrong?" someone asks

"GIGO," the analyst grumbles.

I'd like to reposition and refresh this thinking as—*The Golden Rule of Data.* Do upon your data as you would have it do upon you.

No matter what the Persona at the C-level, no matter what the department and the prevailing system that drives that department, all of them need structured managed data content. So, garbage into Customer Relationship Management (CRM)? You get a bad customer experience and missed opportunities. Garbage into Enterprise Resource Planning (ERP)? You have sub-optimal resource planning. Garbage into a FinTech system? You may get a visit from the regulators. Garbage into ML? You get bad robots. Garbage into BI? *BS.* Garbage into AI? *AS!* Artificial Stupidity! No matter how you slice it or dice it, *The Golden Rule of Data* prevails.

Once upon a time

Your data management story begins with why your company exists. What does your business do? At its essence, every business wants to *deliver value to their relationships through its brands at scale*. Whether you are in banking or manufacturing or a media company or a digital startup, that is what you are trying to do. You have relationships, and you have brands. You want those brands to bring value to your relationships. That is the whole point of business.

Now take that apart and ask: do we have the data behind those ideas? How good is the data you have for those relationships? Customer, vendor, partner, prospect, citizen, patient, or consumer. On the brand side, it is a product, service, offering, banner, asset, or location. Those are all classic master data domains. So instead of saying, "we need to improve the quality of our customer and vendor master," turn the conversation around. Focus on the initiatives you have in the organization to build and strengthen your relationships, transform your customer experience, or move to an as-a-service offering.

These big ideas often require the approval of the executive team. As a data management leader, you have to show that you need the data to back those up. Do you want to transform your customer experience? Let's talk about that. What does that mean to you? Better, deeper engagement?

Predictive assortment? Dynamic pricing? Whatever that means, there is a data piece to it. There is data on customers that probably is not very good because you have duplicates. There is data on brands and products that are spread all over the organization and incomplete. If the organization's strategic intent is to grow through new transformational experiences, you cannot do it unless you have the data foundation.

Most data management messaging focuses on features rather than benefits. Reduce duplicates, improve poor quality data, create a golden record, build a 360-view of the customer or product. Better decision-making, regulatory compliance, effective prioritization, increasing shareholder value—these are nice, but frankly, they can sound generic. Most business stakeholders don't care about these features. They always have the same question:

Why should I care?

Why you need a data story about Why

In his book, *Start with Why,* Simon Sinek states, "People don't buy what you do; they buy why you do it." Sinek didn't come up with the idea of WHY, but he did a great job popularizing it. His audience is mostly consumer marketers and brands, but the same holds for enterprise leadership that needs to support the use of data. Although *WHY* is the most crucial question in business, data discussions at enterprises tend to be predominantly about the *HOW: how* something will be architected, *how* this API connects to that one, *how* it all works. When a business leader asks about *why* something will drive their business, the data person will invariably show them a massive architectural schematic, a bursting chrysanthemum visualization, or a dizzying array of flow diagrams—which rarely explains WHY.

There is a balance, but there is also an order. If you want to understand or articulate the value of data for your organization, and you can't express the WHY first, then the HOW will never matter.

I have had CEOs interrupt me and ask, "why are you telling me this?" Beware of the most show-stopping question of all—*Why should I care?* If this happens to you, you better be ready with an answer.

If you are like most data leaders, you are frustrated that your management doesn't understand. The industry analysts may confound you. Tool vendors and consultants may have burned you. You are sick of banging your head against the wall. And when your time finally comes to make your case, you blow it.

So, let us start over. Once upon a time…

CHAPTER 3

Everyone's Data Story

Here is a data story

Welcome to Enterprise City, a Utopia of interoperability where insight flows seamlessly from workflow to edge across integrated ecosystems. But it wasn't always like this.

Not long ago, Enterprise City was stuck in a Time of Legacy. Separated and attacked by SILOS.

Confused and distracted by MISINFORMATION! Flooded with DUPLICATES that over-ran even the simplest of files! And no SINGLE SOURCE OF TRUTH found anywhere!! In this most desperate time of disparate data, a new hero arose. It was the hero Enterprise City needed. Someone we've always been familiar with but never knew.

All across Enterprise City, everything anyone did turned to data. Businesses would suddenly transform from analog to digital. And instead of fabulous insight, it was nothing but chaos! To tame this overwhelming volume, velocity, and variety of data, emerged MASTER DATA wielding its greatest weapon...THE TRUTH.

When SILOS severed relationships, MASTER DATA enabled integration and interoperability. When DUPLICATES swarmed databases, MASTER DATA uniquely resolved their identity. When MISINFORMATION led to poor business decisions, MASTER DATA fueled irrefutable insight. MASTER DATA brought structure to the unstructured in every part of Enterprise City.

So, when silos, duplicates, and misinformation threaten. Call for MASTER DATA. Boldly laying the foundation for the data-driven and bringing truth and meaning throughout your enterprise. And everyone in Enterprise City loved and trusted their data and worked happily ever after.

Is that how you tell your data story? Probably not. Perhaps a little over-dramatic for most boardrooms, but if you are like many of the thousands of data professionals I have met over my career, you certainly have that type of passion, enthusiasm, and belief in the power and value of well-managed data.

There have been data problems since there was data. Challenges in collecting, understanding, and integrating data are as old as data itself. As Jason Foster of Cynozure once told me, "You can't buy Customer 360, you must build it." There is no silver bullet for a golden record. But there should be some comfort to know that the underlying data issues you have are not particular to any type of company or any vertical or category, and hardly based on location or region. "If you are working in an enterprise, you have enterprise data," said Doug Kimball of Stibo Systems. "If you have enterprise data, then you have enterprise data problems."

This situation is real across every enterprise. Why? Perhaps, it helps to provide some general context for why we got to where we are today. I consider this Everyone's Data Story. These next few sections feature a genericized articulation of the most common data situations. If you find yourself in any of these, and this text helps, please use it to help tell your story. You can't steal it from me because I am giving it to you.

Common problems, same solution, separate pain

Inside the walls of enterprise businesses, various circumstances emphasize the need for data management. These include a significant increase in new data, the changing role of business software systems, miscommunication among employees in different departments, uneven delivery from third-party data services, and a lack of data management standards. These situations can result in organizational disharmony and missed business opportunities.

You have different systems: sales, marketing, finance, operations, among others. You have different regions. You might be local. You might be global. You might be multi-national. You have different go-to-markets. The more complicated your go-to-market, the more data there is about it, and the less consistent that data will be. And finally, you have more and more data coming from third parties. The classic challenge is:

Multiple systems and workflows
Create disparate data
With different definitions
That lack internal standards.

It's everywhere. If you feel this and think it is particular to your vertical or specific to your business, it is everywhere.

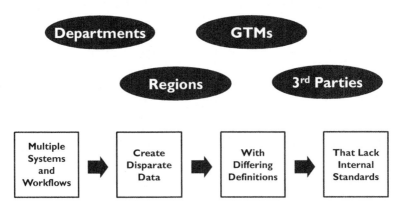

Figure 6 Classic Data Challenge.

Foundational master data is the necessary information on relationships and brands shared across all internal systems, applications, and processes for your commercial data, transactional reporting, and business activity to be optimized and accurate. Because individual businesses and departments need to plan, execute, monitor, and analyze these collective entities, multiple versions of the same data can reside in separate departmental systems. This results in disparate data, difficult to integrate across functions, and quite costly to manage resources and IT development.

Cross-channel initiatives, buying and planning, merger and acquisition activity, and content management are just a few ways new data silos emerge. Significant strategic endeavors, part of any business intelligence strategy, can be hampered or stalled if fundamental master data is not in place. In reality, master data is the only way to connect multiple systems and processes, both internally and externally.

Let's go a bit deeper into understanding the broader business context. During this time of innovation and disruption, business professionals are practically incapable of tracking and measuring activity within and across a multitude of disciplines and channels because there are no implementable standards for data management. Externally, companies impose their structured and unstructured data on their trading partners, leaving each one to bear the continual burden of applying resources to reconcile the differences.

The underlying concept of data management, and especially master data, is surprisingly and deceptively simple. Let's get everyone "on the same page" by having business data and its organization in software systems governed by standards that enable a consistent method for data entry and reporting accuracy. This has never been more important to enterprises. The opportunity of the changing marketing, media, and distribution landscape offers a multitude of means for connecting and engaging with customers and consumers across the spectrum of daily life. Campaign execution and audience insights inform future investments for the correct mix of media and other marketing programs. These insights require rigorous data management practices to be meaningful and reliable. Therefore, the challenge before enterprises is to capitalize on the new landscape through a consistent approach to reap the insights and benefits.

Across every industry, thousands of departmental software systems help plan, execute, and monitor commercial activity. Whether packaged or custom, these solutions were designed to address portions of a business process for a specific department or use case and without an enterprise-wide, much less an industry-standard, reference point.

Within and outside of enterprise boundaries, data alignment among business partners is fundamental to individual and collective objectives. However, with so many conflicting stakeholders within a business and among trading partners, collecting, acquiring, and maintaining foundational data is a complicated endeavor. Brands want a holistic picture of marketing execution to ensure the most correct and effective use of media. They want to understand their supply chain across an array of partners—both vendors and customers. Everyone wants better results, more granular insights, and stricter accountability. Leaders from all parts of the value chain want to know, "How do we get better at providing the right value at the right time in the right context?"

When you consider the competitive and dynamic nature of business today, the need for data management becomes readily apparent. There is a tidal wave of innovation in customer engagement through social media and mobile devices, much of which contains inherently unstructured and disconnected information relating to brands in all kinds of contexts. For example, an automobile manufacturer might run brand imagery creative on a national basis and support it with local media highlighting promotions at individual dealerships. Or a carbonated beverage brand advertising on a national sports championship broadcast will coordinate with local retailers for support on specific package sizes in individual stores. Both brands might use digital, outdoor, in-store, radio, cable, broadcast, print, and mobile advertising across multiple markets.

There are three main parties in these campaigns: the media, the advertising agency, and the brand marketer.

For the Media, where the message is placed, disparate systems can make it extremely difficult to propose and prove the performance of a multichannel package and win more budget share for future campaigns. For each marketing campaign execution, data exists in software systems about customers, vendors, brands, media vehicles, contracts, line-item transactions, creative assets, audience demographics, programming characteristics, and much more.

For the Advertising Agency, which plans and transacts on behalf of the Brand Marketer, disparate systems can interfere with efficient and effective use of an advertising budget—often, this goes unrecognized for months after the campaign concludes. Larger advertising holding companies offer a broad array of services and insights about brands, but they also struggle to aggregate and integrate that data and activity into a standard format.

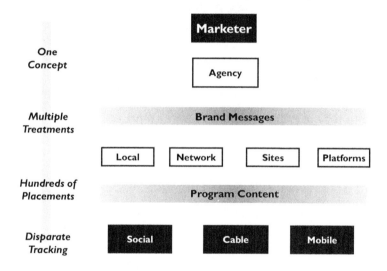

Figure 7 A single brand campaign can be difficult to track and evaluate due to multiple treatments executed through hundreds or thousands of placements across disparate platforms.

For the Brand Marketer, it remains complicated to gauge the individual and cumulative effects of marketing spending on sales. It is difficult to quickly pull together a cross-media report that correctly aligns the campaign information and provides an accurate view of activity.

Even one campaign for one brand can create lots of data problems.

Data explosion

Walk into any enterprise, and you will soon observe that all departments are overwhelmed by an explosion of new data to process and analyze. This results from an ever-evolving demand for more refined insights from distribution channels, the growing variety of media platforms, and a nearly infinite number of consumer and industrial devices.

Companies have invested a great deal of technology and resources in analytics systems required for business reporting. Many analytics projects drag on for years, yield a fraction of expected insights, or are scaled back, in large part due to the challenge of aligning disparate data across systems. To obtain full value from analytics initiatives, you must place greater or equal importance on data management.

Business stakeholders have alarmingly low levels of confidence in the integrity and accuracy of the data. For global enterprises, this is an untenable situation where insights into business fundamentals are not attainable without a significant application of human resources to collate information manually.

The role of enterprise software systems

Enterprise software systems reflect the business needs that existed when the systems were created. Consider, for example, the analogy of an automobile's longevity versus value: If properly cared for, the car can run almost indefinitely. But over time, needs change, and the vehicle's fundamental purpose no longer meets the capability requirements. The family might grow; the need for more comfort might increase; the environmental priorities and awareness might change, resulting in the acquisition of a new vehicle. In the enterprise world, it is not uncommon for companies to be using software applications architected and built when the purpose and scope of need were far different from today.

Also, it is widespread for individual business departments and primary functions within a given enterprise to use various software and manual methods to track the business lifecycle for the same entity. For example, enterprises run concurrent systems and processes for finance, sales, fulfillment, and shipping, where there is no standard vocabulary and alignment for business management. Intermediaries such as agencies, brokers, and distributors, have stand-alone applications for research, planning, buying, production, traffic, finance, client management, and other stewardship activities. The media implements multiple systems for sales representatives, agency-advertiser relationships, traffic, billing, and creative placement. Around these core systems are many stand-alone systems that help departments overcome functional limitations. This arrangement usually results in one-way relationships that yield even more data fragmentation and limited usability—and thus low value in terms of feeding insights for the opportunity, risk, and profitability.

While these legacy systems may continue to support critical workloads, they are inherently flawed. These systems, designed for a specific and limited purpose or scope, are often built with technology on a foundation that limits options for extensibility and meets evolving business requirements. Perhaps the most fundamental issue is that the business stakeholders most likely did not support standards for defining and managing data and likewise did not carry any standards forward as other systems propagated across the company. Most large companies are held captive by the limitations of their legacy technology systems. The most desirable way out of the problem is to build another—sowing the self-fulfilling result of increasingly fragmented data.

Moving it all to the cloud or a data lake does not replace the underlying need for data management. In some respects, the cloud can simply be considered a place to store and access data. It is as if one took all their personal belongings from a basement, attic, and closets, and dumped it into a third-party rented storage bin. All their junk is undoubtedly more accessible and in one place, but it is still a lot of unsorted junk.

Organizational disharmony

People across departments work in different and legacy systems across their enterprise. As you can imagine, different views from different data about the same business activity can be a significant source of stress for individual contributors to an overall business process. How often have you witnessed a discussion between two department workers who cannot match what they see in their individual systems? All disciplines have their perspectives, and tensions are inevitable when each discipline assumes its viewpoint is the only correct one.

All enterprises face extreme data management and reporting challenges. Many have grown through years of business and brand acquisitions. These acquired or merged companies may align with their new parent at the strategic level, but rarely at the data layer. As the years pass, few can transition to a unified set of data. The inability to take on new economies of scale and expand market presence is due, in part, to a lack of unified data governance, which leads to duplicate master, reference, and metadata.

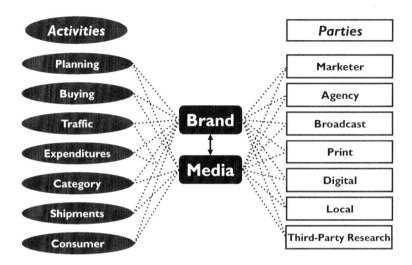

Figure 8 Different data on the same business activity can be a source of stress for business stakeholders.

Instead of implementing a systems-based solution, individual efforts often compensate for any data misalignments and gaps. As any industry evolves in terms of information and complexity, you need more than an analyst role to fix problems—you also must involve more senior levels, as governance and compliance requirements demand.

This change is time-consuming and requires thoughtful execution—making it stressful for anyone involved. Leadership, often shielded from the clerical effort undertaken to fix differences among organization silos, might mandate a balance across various systems. Mistakes can snowball into considerable discrepancies.

Impact of third-party data providers

Third-party research, tracking, alternative data, and analytics providers are not immune to data management challenges of their own. Syndicated research providers measure audience exposure to media content, track product movement, purchase dynamics, and advertising expenditures for branded messages. They can provide intent data about buying preferences, metrics, insights, and analysis. Like their clients, these providers maintain separate market or tracking services with multiple nomenclature schemes for brands, relationship types, and media vehicles.

With each new market research and alternative-data provider comes yet another set of taxonomies, hierarchies, and geography definitions. A new service rarely adopts a standard for integration with their clients. Rarer still for there to be a centralized body that aligns this type of data to a unifying standard.

The increased focus on both pay-for-performance and as-a-service models suggests that, besides the demand for a back-to-basics business metrics approach, there is an unwillingness to pay a service provider overhead expense for data aggregation and reporting.

Enterprises continually press third-party data suppliers for deeper and more profound analytics that drive tangible business results. However, their disparate array of services makes it difficult for these third-party data suppliers to provide integrated insights to their clients. Dissatisfaction grows as these external sources provide inconsistent definitions and limited integration. Also, many global market research suppliers have expanded by acquisition, presenting another level of challenge.

One notable exception is the Nielsen Connected Partner Program. They have partner research providers who align their data at the product and location dimensions to ease integration for the end-users. The structure for the location dimension is based on the TDLinx service I brought to market nearly 25 years ago. It is heartwarming to know that my pioneering work is still as relevant as ever.

Lack of data management standards

At a time when enterprises across a value chain most need to manage and understand their business on a holistic basis to grow, there is a lack of industry reference standards for data recording and management. Without the benefit of shared master data as a tangible output of data management, software solution developers have created business systems with their own data definitions or definitions supplied to them to meet departmental criteria. For example, a system may not have incorporated governance controls to reduce records duplication based on inconsistent naming conventions. As a result, the information and data output of these systems may render rich details but cannot accurately summarize activity, even for a single entity.

This lack of standardized data is a major stumbling block for those who have invested, and continue to spend, substantial resources in IT initiatives to build integrated distribution, marketing, and management solutions. Major projects like enterprise resource planning (ERP), customer relationship management (CRM), MarTech, media and production transactional systems, business synchronization platforms, and the developing arenas of customer data platforms (CDP) and content management systems (CMS) offer great strategic benefits. Across the enterprise spectrum, there is a constant conflict between the implementation of new enterprise systems and the foothold of long-established legacy and custom applications. An unfortunate by-product of the implementation of many systems is the creation of yet another data silo.

These multiple systems and separate processes create disparate data and conflicting hierarchies. This leads to a lack of integration and flawed reporting, misaligned goals between partners, difficulty determining ROI, reduced confidence in data quality, and general marketplace dissonance.

The "outside the walls" problem

Outside the walls of your organization, business trade between enterprises adds even more complications. Proprietary views run rampant not only within the enterprises themselves but also across and between partners. This lack of alignment compounds the problem as each separate party maintains incongruent definitions and conflicting hierarchies. Many opportunities exist to reduce the cost of trading between partners. Still, without a concerted effort to drive standard data management practices, the contractual lifecycle and interactions will continue to be redundant, labor-intensive, and susceptible to errors.

This is all symptomatic of significant, disabling forces that fundamentally contribute to many a vision going unfulfilled. The foundation can hardly sustain the enterprise in the current environment, much less provide a platform for future initiatives. It should become apparent that an effective corporate strategy depends upon a sound data management program.

****

Others can help you with culture change and organizational structure. But without a common understanding of the data management problem and a clear narrative about the solution, cultures don't change, and organizations are dysfunctional.

In light of the tremendous growth in platforms and the concurrent explosion of data sources, enterprises, and their partners, cannot profitably and efficiently manage business without a sustainable data management program. The market, relationships, and future growth prospects will continue to suffer from manual, ad-hoc, and non-integrated processes that waste resources and impede the path to implementation and efficiency.

A data management program that is well planned and executed within individual companies strengthens all parts of the value chain: customers, suppliers, distributors as well as the third-party research and service providers that support them. Data management can touch and improve every transaction, plan, analysis, and budget. Conversely, organizations that lack data management likely will continue on an ever-deepening spiral of siloed, segregated, and inflexible business processes.

The key to consistently harnessing the value of data is to establish and define a data management program. With proper executive support, this data management program can lead your organization on the journey to a synchronized, well-functioning network of better data. The data management program ensures a technology-based solution for setting and enforcing internal standards, a business taxonomy that supports connectivity, and adherence to the common data across all systems.

CHAPTER 4

Framing Your Data Story

In this section, let's break it all down into some simple, business-accessible organizational nuggets that you can use to frame your story. These are not operational frameworks or consultative maturity models, but they are road-tested conversational approaches to help articulate the objectives and challenges every enterprise faces when it comes to data.

These frameworks are:

- The 3 Phases of Digital Transformation
- The 4Cs of Data Structure
- The 8 'Ates of Using Data

As you read them, think about how they might apply to your business. Which phase of digital transformation are you in? Do the 4Cs apply to the data structure you have for your relationships and brands? I discovered that every way an enterprise uses data is covered in The 8' Ates. Do they sound familiar? Are there more? I haven't found any.

The data story of digital transformation

Digital transformation is part of a burning platform for every modern enterprise. Digital transformation can mean different things to different people. Still, one thing it means to every single enterprise is: you have more data now than you ever had before, and you have to find new ways to manage it that you never thought of before, so you can do things you never dreamed of before.

There are broader political and cultural business dynamics inherent in digital transformation. Yet, the nature of data creation, management, curation, and integration will determine the success or failure of each enterprise. Some businesses will transform and deliver a staggering increase of value in new markets, while others will find themselves isolated as they confront the possibility of extinction. Going forward, how you manage, master, and structure your data will determine if you become empowered or devoured by digital transformation.

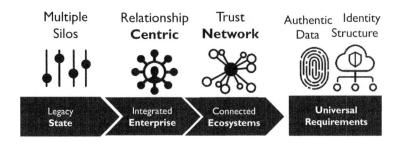

Figure 9 The Three Phases of Digital Transformation.

Those who succeed in harnessing these advancements at scale will flourish. Their success will spawn disruptive innovation, new levels of customer experience, and unprecedented business value. Those who cannot leverage these new ideas could find themselves stuck in a legacy quagmire of inefficiency and abrupt market irrelevance that will ultimately lead to their demise. The one constant in all this disruption is data.

Digital transformation is a combination of people, technology, process, and data. As a data professional, you need to understand and articulate why *data management is the foundation of digital transformation*. There is a common need for data management at every enterprise that embarks on a digital transformation journey.

Businesses tend to move along a similar path on their digital transformation journey from a legacy state of *multiple silos,* toward an integrated enterprise embracing *relationship centricity,* then outward as a part of a connected ecosystem in a *trust network.* The terminology for each of these phases may differ by vertical—the process to move from one step to another could have very different challenges. The typical journey, however, runs through these three common phases.

- **Phase 1**. Acknowledge the LEGACY STATE of MULTIPLE SILOS. Sales, marketing, finance, operations, and other systems do not seamlessly connect at the data layer.

- **Phase 2**. Achieve RELATIONSHIP CENTRICITY in an INTEGRATED ENTERPRISE. These holistic steps are necessary to put business relationships at the center—both strategically and systematically—of enterprise activity.

- **Phase 3**. Engage with TRUST NETWORKS across CONNECTED ECOSYSTEMS. Data-sharing consortiums, channel partner platforms, e-commerce customer self-service, supplier on-boarding programs, and dependency on vertical industry identifiers/standards (LEI, UPC/GTIN, Ad-ID).

Phase 1 – A legacy state of multiple silos

As businesses strive to drive innovation and progress, they continue to grow in complexity and foster fragmentation. The explosion of persona-based tech stacks (ERP, CRM, CDP, FinTech, MarTech, AdTech, etc.) offers unprecedented flexibility, but inherent in each new app is yet another silo. In each silo, there is the potential to create another version of the same data. Separate departments, regions, channels, and go-to-markets create separate data.

Globalization and frequent merger and acquisition activity tend to increase these operational barriers and create an inability to scale. Vital relationship types (such as customer, vendor, partner, and prospect), as well as other essential brand entities (like product, service, and offering), often have different definitions across different parts of the same organization.

For example, the CRM used by a local sales team might define a *customer* as individual locations. Simultaneously, the global finance department may view this same customer's full hierarchy as a single entity. Both interpretations may be correct in their respective contexts but appear inaccurate and irrelevant to each other, and in most cases, they are not in sync. Imagine the frustration of that customer whose experience is negatively impacted by this lack of synchronization. They have two salespeople calling on them at the same time. Or their pricing and credit status isn't reflected across the entire relationship. Your customer-facing resources are wasted explaining the results of bad data instead of improving the experience.

A legacy state creates a drag on all data-oriented processes and endeavors. An excellent proof of concept designed in a silo may never be able to scale. Frustration builds while different departments have limited and inaccurate views of relationships and brands.

External reputations suffer when the enterprise cannot provide, react, interpret, or even determine a holistic view of a given relationship. A long-time customer mistakenly treated as a new prospect. A bad-debt relationship suddenly takes advantage of terms they should never have received. Products are not in stock, and deliveries are delayed. Executives are befuddled by different numbers.

Most enterprises are in some form of this legacy state. This does not mean they do not have modern technology and infrastructure. This simply means that they have not taken the holistic steps necessary to put relationships and brands at the center of their processes—both strategically and systematically. To move out to this legacy state, you need to establish a common foundation across these silos.

Phase 2 – Establishing relationship centricity across an integrated enterprise

Relationships are the basis of all business. Although many organizations think they are "customer-centric," their data can hardly support that notion. Ask yourself: *do your systems know what your people know?* To create innovative experiences that are at the core of digital transformation, enterprises must first embrace being *relationship-centric.* When built upon standard definitions, relationship centricity is a consolidated view of your relationships across the entire enterprise. A familiar approach involves creating a 360-degree view of the customer, vendor, supplier, or partner as well as product, brand, and service.

Compliance efforts such as KYC (Know Your Customer), GDPR (General Data Protection Regulations), and CCPA (California Consumer Protection Act) are among the growing list of data privacy and security regulations. These deepen the requirements for a consistent and shared view and definition of each unique relationship. Development activities like cross-sell/up-sell and the foundation of any ABM (Account-Based Marketing) program are on a stable, shared definition of "account." This idea of the integrated enterprise, of being centric about relationships, is only achieved by establishing and governing a common version of the truth about those relationships.

This does not mean everyone needs to have access to everything all the time. That is neither practical nor necessary. But it does mean the data about relationships and brands must be trusted by the organization. Definitions, hierarchies, taxonomies, and other fundamental structural elements can no longer be a topic for on-going debate. Although finance and legal may require a different view of a relationship than sales and marketing, those two views should be synchronized. The ability to disassemble and reassemble these views to serve each constituency is critical.

This is particularly important when leveraging technologies and methods used by advanced analytics. Data scientists, data engineers, DataOps, and other data consumers should spend their time using, understanding, and leveraging data instead of doubting its origin and integrity.

Phase 3 — Engage in trust networks through connected ecosystems

Once relationship centricity is embraced and becomes stable inside your enterprise, you need to look outward and participate in some form of a trust network. A trust network is how you engage, interoperate, and seamlessly communicate with different parties across your value chains. Using the same standard data and definitions, or links to the same authoritative data and definitions, across verticals and markets provides the basis for seamless integration.

This can manifest itself in channel partner platforms, e-commerce, customer self-service, supplier on-boarding systems, vertical industry identifiers/standards, such as UPC (Universal Product Code), GTIN (Global Trade Identification Number), Ad-ID (Advertising Identifier), and LEI (Legal Entity Identifier). When you transform your business model from selling a tangible widget to licensing that widget's value through a subscription as-a-service, you establish a new type of trust network.

Ecosystems can only reach their full potential when built on accuracy and trust. In many cases, our business dealings are based on personal feelings. Good faith can sour quickly if the data supporting that relationship is inaccurate, outdated, and unstructured. Leveraging common data and syndicated processes between external parties allow the interoperability in a trust network to scale.

Universal requirements for digital transformation

In a digitally-transformed organization, data moves seamlessly from workflow to workflow and between external partners. Organizations move from legacy silos to being relationship-centric and then to part of a trust network. Users can be confident in the analytics and spend their time improving the relationship experience rather than questioning the data.

Since digital transformation runs on data, properly managing the diverse types and profuse quantities of that data will directly impact an organization's ability to succeed and survive. Creating a common protocol at the semantic layer for relationship and brand entities provides a much quicker time to value for any kind of enterprise data management and interoperability initiative. Standardized, expertly-governed master, reference, and metadata content can seamlessly integrate internally across methodologies, processes, workflows, apps, and platforms, as well as externally between enterprises, value chains, and throughout market ecosystems. Think of it as a common language for customers, vendors, partners, prospects, brands, products, services, assets, and offerings.

The consistent and universal requirements for progress along this three-phase journey are *authenticated identity* and a *common data structure*. Achieving semantic consistency through data management enables faster integration and deeper interoperability at ever-increasing levels. This is a relevant value proposition for all commercial, educational and governmental enterprises.

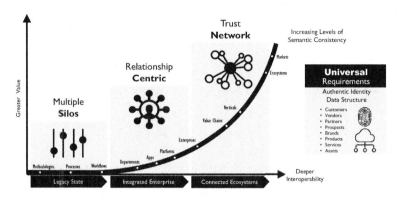

Figure 10 Increasing levels of semantic consistency enables the journey through the phases of digital transformation.

Legacy State	Integrated Enterprise	Connected Ecosystems
Separate Systems	360° View of X	Vertical Standards
Disparate Data	Golden Record	Global Master Brands
Differing Definitions	Shared Version of the Truth	Connected Commerce
Lack of Standards	Trusted Identity/KYC	Automated CX
Operational Barriers	Globalization/M&A	Immutable Ledgers
Inability to Scale	ABM Strategy	Internet of Things (IoT)
Business Disruption	ML & AI	4th Industrial Revolution
MULTIPLE SILOS	**RELATIONSHIP CENTRIC**	**TRUST NETWORK**

Figure 11 Mission-critical priorities and characteristics.

The story of structured data – 4Cs

Data management program leaders must have governance over—and market expertise on—the universal business data that exist throughout the value chain. Seemingly tactical activities, such as normalizing naming conventions, applying consistent identification keys and codes, and correcting hierarchical assignments, are the foundational data building blocks for achieving a successful data management program. The data management practice is the central point of management and control for a unified company nomenclature.

To find the value data has to offer, it must be structured. It must align across disparate sources so that you can extract and distill the most useful and relevant information. It is the differentiator between a flood of unstructured and disparate information and a standardized and structured data source that everyone can trust. What makes Big Data "big" is its lack of structure. Most, if not all, standardized executive and activity reporting comes from structured data.

Structured data works harder than unstructured data.

Applying structure is difficult and time-consuming. It can be fraught with debates about the *structure* of the structure itself. That means you need to do the hard work of defining and gaining consensus on important terms like *customer, brand,* and *market.* But without those basics, the rest is a mess.

Structured data in the form of master, reference, and metadata is the most important data any organization has.

It is the data in charge of your business. Since it is about your relationships and brands, is there anything more important in your business? No. So the logic follows that the data about those relationships and brands is your most important data.

All the other data is *about* the structured data. Until you have the foundational structure set, the common definitions established, and the processes in place to govern both of those, you will be tossed and turned on a sea of disparate data. The structure of your data, or lack of it, causes many issues with reporting and analytics. The usual complaints about data include:

- Why don't we have a list of top customers?
- This hierarchy is wrong.
- Look at all these duplicates!
- These products are missing.
- What do we mean by this market?

Some in the analytics community may disagree and believe that unstructured and semi-structured data hold the most valuable insights. Unstructured data offers loads of analytical promise, insight, and value—but you need structured data first for your organization. An insurance company getting flooded with mobile-phone pictures of accidents needs to have machine learning and artificial intelligence processes to interpret these unstructured inputs. If their machine learning algorithms don't recognize a *front left fender* as a *front left fender*, the service will not be accurate.

Applying structure to unstructured data is how value is released. But before you can do the cool stuff, you need to do that hard work. As Pink Floyd (and your mother) reminds us—*You can't have your pudding if you don't eat your meat.* Structured data is all meat. Despite all the clamor and celebration of unstructured and semi-structured data, the basics are still the basics. While data scientists spin their graphs and search for analytical needles in their big data haystack, the business needs answers. Answers to questions like:

- How many customers do we have?
- Are sales up?
- Have we increased market share?
- Where do we deploy media?
- Which partners are the most effective?

If structured data is about your relationships and your brands in the beginning, where do you begin this beginning? How do you structure these relationships? How do you start to codify these relationships? And most importantly, in the context of Telling Your Data Story, can you convince your business stakeholders to take this seriously?

Let's go back to the subject of most data—*relationships* and *brands*. Relationship and brand data are most often organized by segmentation, aligned by hierarchy, and viewed by geography. A simple concept to describe the basic structure needed for your relationship and brand data are The 4Cs: Code, Company, Category, and Country.

- A CODE lets you know something is unique
- A COMPANY lets you know who owns it
- A CATEGORY lets you know what kind of relationship it is
- A COUNTRY lets you know where it is

Code – Is it unique?

Every record about a relationship and a brand in a database has a code—somewhere. You need some form of unique identifier—a customer code, a record ID, a product code. *"I have a code. Therefore, I am."* in a database. Once a code is put on a record—it "exists" in that database. You need a code to make sure it is unique. But since every system has its own set of codes, you probably have more than one across your multiple workflows, departments, and regions.

You may have issues with duplicate codes or two different codes on what ends up being the same entity. For example, a *sales record* and a *billing record* for the same customer may exist in two different systems. Linking those codes or deciding which one to replace with the other is an essential aspect of data governance. If you can tie these codes together, that is your shortest path to a comprehensive and standard version of that relationship. There is plenty of expert advice on *reconciling, matching, de-duplicating, managing* survivorship, and more, to solve this issue. But business leaders may not even understand why there is a code in the first place.

There is nothing unique about a unique identifier

Some third-party data providers believe their code is the only code you will ever need. This is never true. You will always need an internal code for your system and your workflows. The identification of an entity is something you must own within your data governance program. You can undoubtedly validate and enrich the relationship or brand entity with third-party data. Still, it is dangerous to believe that an external party will care more about your data than you do.

Many individual standards bodies require a particular code to identify entities in transactions regardless of your internal code. There are subsets of ecosystems that identify entities among each other with standard or syndicated codes. CDQ (Corporate Data Quality), a Switzerland-based enterprise data sharing community, tracks more than 400 official legal, governmental, and financial unique identifiers. Unfortunately, there is no single universally-accepted, unique identifier that works globally across all systems. I have yet to find a dependable service or source that can manage the significant interoperability and integration challenges that this presents.

Example of Unique Identifiers for Coca-Cola		
Type	Source	Code
UPC	GSI	049000
Ticker	NYSE	KO
CUSIP	S&P	191098102
PermID	Refinitiv	4295903091
LEI	GLEIF	UWJKFUJFZ02DKWI3RY53
DUNS	D&B	003296175
Factual ID	Factual	d6c31c17-bf79-47ad-9d45-8bacaac6dc45
Tax ID	IRS	580503352
Open FIGI	Bloomberg	BBG000FBVT91
Ad-ID	4As/ANA	LP

Figure 12 As they say, the beauty of standards is that there are so many to choose from.

Company – Who owns it?

You need to know *whom an entity belongs to* through a hierarchical structure, often known as a parent/child relationship or family tree. A hierarchy has multiple levels, from the local branch, divisions, subsidiaries, all the way up to an ultimate global parent. *Bill-to, ship-to, plan-to, sell-to* are all part of the hierarchy. The bigger the relationship, the more complicated the hierarchy.

Are you engaging with all the relevant divisions or branches of a given family tree? Do you have a relationship with it already? Is it related to something that increases your risk? Are there business terms you would apply because of that ownership? Simple cross-sell/up-sell activities are impossible if you do not maintain a full hierarchy of a relationship.

Similarly, brands have an ownership hierarchy. A product may be a variant of a brand, which is part of a larger franchise. Think of *Coke, Diet Coke,* and *Diet Caffeine-Free Cherry Vanilla Coke.* Those are all parts of the same Coca-Cola parent brand franchise. Some products may have a different brand name depending on the country but still belong to the same parent brand. For example, *Diet Coke* in the United States is known as *Coke-Lite* in Europe.

Different hierarchies can co-exist within an enterprise: legal, financial, sales, operations, marketing. Every enterprise needs to find a way to create a total commercial view to consistently aggregate all of their activity with their most significant relationships. This is generally for the *CEO-to-CEO Lunch Meeting* use case. During a typical top-to-top meeting, executives want a sense of the complete relationship. Unfortunately, there is no syndicated way to create these views.

Most business reporting includes some form of hierarchy. Get those standard definitions straight, eliminate extraneous views, and you are closer to the clarity your business needs. Challenge the request for too many particular hierarchies or exclusive views used by a single department or associate. But reinforcing to the business that hierarchy is essential is the first step.

Category – What is it?

You need to know what *kind* of thing you are dealing with, especially if you don't have much of a relationship with it. Categories define market share, TAMs (total addressable markets), enable segmentation, and are the denominator for penetration analysis. Category attributes determine targeting. You try to find likely prospects based on industry, segment, or sub-segment.

We are successful with this kind of company. I need to find more of that kind of company.

Many enterprises deploy their sales and marketing efforts by industry type or vertical segments. If the category structure is weak or confusing or missing, then these sales and marketing efforts are at best sub-optimized and, at worst, a complete waste.

Category attributes drive procurement and sourcing. You look to find potential suppliers based on industry, segment, or sub-segment. It is essential to leverage a standardized category structure wherever possible and practical. Categorization is critical when bringing together different relationships or brands into a common, broader view. There are often industry-standard classification schemes and common definitions. Some are better than others, but they all support the notion that you must determine an entity type. There are considerable granularity and nuances to categories: types and sub-types, channels and sub-channels, segment and sub-segments, genres, and sub-genres.

Your category structure will depend entirely on your business needs. Some industries have rigorous categorization requirements based on accepted industry standards. Some manufacturers have ten or even fifteen levels of categorization they use for internal analysis and planning. Some may only have three. The higher the level of the category, the easier it is to define. Remember the children's guessing game: *animal vegetable, mineral*? It starts with high-level groupings. How you structure and what standards you use for your categorization are up to you and your stakeholders. But you must have a category to know what type of entity you have. People can play all sorts of games with categories. They create misleading reporting and analytics to suggest, "we are number one in our category, which we define as *us* followed by everyone smaller than *us*."

"Other" almost always a "Top 10" category

Look at the bottom of your reports. If you dig deep enough, you will probably find a category you called

Other. If you are not diligent, it could become one of your fastest-growing segments. My favorite is *Other/Other*.

When asked why a database has *Other/Other*, it is generally because the users have trouble spelling *miscellaneous*! You will often find *NULL, NA, missing,* and various types of filler data in the category field. I once saw the attribute value *DK*. When asked what that stood for, they said, "don't know."

Country – Where is it?

Following along our alliteration with Cs, you also need *country* and some form of geography. Geography has a hierarchy too—region, province, city, zip, or postal code. The media market, sales market, and measurement market are different configurations of geography depending on your use case. Similar to a category, geography determines sales assignments and media placements. It is the market in market share. But agreeing on a standard definition of the market will clear up lots of confusion between departments when you simply ask, "How am I doing in *New York Metro* or *All Major Markets* or EMEA?"

The 4Cs make lots of data problems go away

Imagine how well your data would flow if you knew you had unique records (code), that every one of them had a full and updated hierarchy (company), complete segmentation (category), and consistent geographic information (country and market). This creates a common language between departments about simple but vital elements of your business relationships. WHERE something is, WHAT it is. WHO owns it and that it is UNIQUE.

The 4Cs are also the basis of your essential business vocabulary. I will cover the importance of vocabulary in a later chapter. The 4Cs represent the characters in your data story: *Entities, Hierarchies, Segments,* and *Geographies.* Depending on your business dynamics, you might call them:

- Outlet, Account, Channel, Market
- Item, Supplier, Sector, Region
- Product, Brand, Segment, Market
- Matter, Client, Type, Office
- Consumer, Household, Demographic, Metro Area

If you can confidently determine where something is, what kind of thing it is, who owns it, and that it is genuinely unique, you can more easily manage your relationships across your company.

Once the data on your relationships and brands is structured and standardized, it can harmonize and integrate better into your processes, methodologies, and workflows between your systems, regions, and go-to-markets-as well as externally within an ecosystem.

CODE	COMPANY	CATEGORY	COUNTRY
Entity	Hierarchy	Sector	Geography
Outlet	Account	Channel	Region
Product	Brand	Segment	Market
Thing	Parent	Type	Place
Unique	Who	What	Where

Figure 13 The 4Cs may go by different names depending on your industry.

As you try to gain a holistic view of your relationships and anticipate future needs, applying these 4Cs will align you to your data objectives more quickly. It will also give you the structure and scalability required for your enterprise data journey. All sorts of data problems go away. Think of all the data projects and analytics efforts that depend on entity uniqueness, standardized hierarchies, consistent segmentation, and precise geographies. Data scientists waste time unduplicating entities, determining hierarchies, and trying to reconcile segmentations and geographies. They call it munging and wrangling.

How many executive decisions are made upon customer counts, family trees, prospect targeting, and market coverage? Many of your data efforts will fall back on disambiguation, hierarchies, segmentation, and geographies. Authenticated identity and determining uniqueness vanish with consistent management of identifiers.

Let's just take a short Zen moment and think about the potential clarity this brings to your data.

Take a moment—deep breath. It feels better just thinking about it.

The story of using data – 8 'Ates

When you need to describe why you use data in your organization, it may help to explain it with some general principles. Here is a series of use cases, notions, ideas, thoughts, and approaches that encompass nearly everything an enterprise would want to do with data. It might seem as though there should be hundreds of them, but I have boiled these down to eight specific concepts called The 8 'Ates. Yes, you may find an edge case here and there. There are always exceptions. But *most* of what you do with *most* of your data *most* of the time to get *most* of the value is covered by these eight activities:

1. Relate
2. Validate
3. Integrate
4. Aggregate
5. Interoperate
6. Evaluate
7. Communicate
8. Circulate

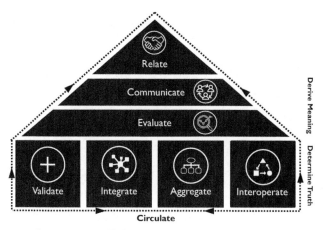

Figure 14 The 8 'Ates—All the ways Enterprises use data.

1. Relate – Grow relationships

How does data enhance my relationships with customers, vendors, and partners?

At the pinnacle is RELATE. Everybody wants to relate. That is what all organizations do. You want to grow relationships. You want to improve your relationships. You want to mitigate the risk of some relationships. You want to stay in compliance with the regulations regarding certain types of relationships. You have to be able to care for those relationships. How do you build a relationship with your customers, prospects, and partners through your brands, products, and services? You want to have all this wonderful data about your relationships to power your organization. If you do not have relationships, you do not have a business.

2. Validate – Establish uniqueness

Is this entity unique? Can I validate its identity? Is it a duplicate?

Before you begin a relationship, you must VALIDATE it. You cannot have a healthy relationship with something unless you know what that thing is. Do I have this relationship already? Do I have an authentic identity? Security is based on a validated identity for a given relationship. Is it trying to trick me? It is trying to be deceptive. It is defunct in some way—out of business, deceased, or no longer active. Should I bring it into my system? Do you have permission and consent to have this relationship? That is an essential factor regarding data privacy. You have to make sure they opt-in depending on what the entity is. It is a similar approach to products and brands. Is this a unique product name? Is this a unique product SKU or item?

Did you disambiguate? Did you search before creating a new record? *Search before create* is a very effective validation process. Simple but hard to execute. For example, how many places in your organization can you create a customer? "Well, we have 28 places to do customer create." You have 28 places to perform *customer creation*? No wonder you have a problem! The more places you have to create a new record, the fewer people will start by *searching* first. Salespeople that are in the field working with customers don't want to spend much time in data management. They add duplicates.

You want to make sure you have that validation process in place before you move forward. That is where a lot of trouble starts. People insert new records and add new relationships without a consistent validation process. You have to stop bad data right at the beginning. The lack of a proper validation process is how garbage gets into your system.

3. Integrate – Data enrichment

Do I have everything I need to know from all available sources?

Then you want to INTEGRATE. You want to take all the disparate sources of data you have and pull them all together in some way. It could be physically. It could be virtually. I won't tell you how to do it, but you want to get everything you know about a thing in a way that it is accessible across your organization.

You need to know as much as you can about whatever that thing is. Then everybody, at every level, has the right view of everything going on. Yes, a noble goal, not everybody is there, but it is happening at the most advanced enterprises.

You may have data from multiple systems and external suppliers. You will want that data integrated. You may have extended attributes, metrics, insight, alerts, and intent from third parties that you use to enrich the data you already have on your entities.

The idea is, "take what I can know about a thing and pull it all together." This is commonly known as some form of *360 view*. A way to get that *Customer 360* or that *Product 360* is to integrate all these disparate data sources.

4. Aggregate – Standardized reporting

Can I roll it up? Can I report across multiple dimensions (geography, hierarchy, category)?

Next, you begin to AGGREGATE. You work at different levels at an enterprise. Ship-to, Bill-to, Plan-to, Sell-to. You want to be able to aggregate all that data up. Much of business reporting starts with aggregating data. How do you pull data together up to the market level, to the company level, to the category level? Most executive reporting is some form of aggregating data to top markets, top accounts, and top segments. These typical levels also drive a lot of integration. Data integration often happens at the aggregate levels of market, customer, or segment.

Here are The 4Cs at work—code, company, category, country—that structure drives so much reporting. What are your top categories? Who are your top customers? Where are your top markets? If you are missing these core dimensions, then you will be missing data in a report. If the business user is familiar with the market conditions and thinks data is missing, that will reduce the trust in that report. Aggregated data is often used to integrate other sources—two of the 'Ates at work. You may have granular data on every entity in a market that needs to be aggregated so you can overlay other information you have at that same market level.

5. Interoperate – Seamless connections

Will it connect to other systems? Can I use it in automated processes?

Then you begin to INTEROPERATE. How do you share data seamlessly across processes? Can you connect machine-to-machine with other parties? Can you speak on a data-to-data basis with other systems that are both within your enterprise and externally outside your enterprise? The act of taking standardized data and putting it into a process allows your business to do things with considerably less effort. Interoperability also will enable you to make decisions at scale. That is what organizations want to do. *Scale* could be the single-word benefit of well-managed data. When you put it into a process, it enables automation. Instead of manually doing something ten times, you can automatically do it a hundred or a thousand or a billion times.

You have to enable interoperability to drive a tremendous amount of value. Most integration of systems happens at the software layer, but you cannot lose sight of interoperability at the data layer. Interoperability is the backbone of many innovative initiatives today. Remember that digital transformation value grows by achieving semantic interoperability at ever-increasing levels.

The UPC – Interoperability in everyday life

A supermarket is a perfect place to see structured data and interoperability in action. Look at the value of the UPC bar code. Take a bottle, box, jar, can, bag, or tube of a product to the cash register. The checkout clerk runs it across the scanner, and it goes "beep." That little "beep" is a machine recognizing the UPC. The product is identifiable because there is highly-structured standardized master and reference data in the point-of-sale system. The system also has the associated price of that item. Hundreds of systems in thousands of stores can recognize millions of items in billions of transactions. This only happens because structured data enables interoperability. Beep!

6. Evaluate – Create insight

What does it mean? Can I analyze it?

VALIDATE, INTEGRATE, AGGREGATE, and INTEROPERATE form the foundation. Those are activities that allow an enterprise to *determine* the truth in their data. Once you have built this foundation, then you can start to EVALUATE. That's where analytics comes in. Then you get into business intelligence, machine learning, and artificial intelligence. Most data scientists are wasting time doing data janitor work cleaning up, munging, and wrangling data. If you don't have a foundation of truth on the bottom, you will not get adequate meaning when you start to evaluate. Until you have done that, the evaluation process is a waste of time. You cannot produce enterprise-grade analytics without a solid data foundation.

Every business intelligence reporting tool I have ever seen demos well because the demo data is perfect. If the data is not perfect, the tool does not work. Don't start pouring data in a fancy visualization tool and do all kinds of crazy reporting until you have the foundational things done. Otherwise, business stakeholders are not going to trust the dashboard you put in front of them. You want to make sure you have standardized, clean, trusted data in your evaluation process. Remember:

Good decisions made on bad data are just bad decisions you don't know about…yet.

---

7. Communicate – Common language

How do we convey meaning to each other?

People in relationships need to COMMUNICATE. They want to make a point. They want to drive a business initiative. Data allows you to communicate across an organization and between parties. You must have common definitions and standard structures before you can have a successful communication process. One of the first exercises in data governance is to create a business glossary with a standardized set of terminology that everyone can use in an enterprise to describe different entities. You want to be able to communicate clearly and consistently with data. Think about the terminology people use in the data space.

- Do we speak the same language?
- Are we on the same page?
- Do we understand each other?

Have you experienced walking into a meeting with a report with one number, and your counterpart across the table has a different number? You say there are nine things, and they say there are 12, and five of them aren't the same. You start arguing about the definitions, and before you know it, the meeting is over. That happens when you do not have a consistent structure underneath that everyone can understand.

You must communicate if you want to have a good relationship.

Just ask anybody you love.

8. Circulate – Data in motion

How is this data shared across my organization?

Data, to have value, must be in motion. Data must CIRCULATE. Data has to move across processes, move across methodologies, move across enterprises, move across verticals, and entire markets. Data cannot hide in a silo. It cannot be locked in a PDF file. People in your organization cannot hold it because they want to keep their job. It cannot be the province of one person who knows how to do that special report that no one else can do. Those days are already over. The reason those people still get to do that special little report is that they haven't been caught yet.

Data must reach the point of decision as quickly as possible. That is, your data must become viable and reliable with little delay. Ensure it becomes available to the right people at the right time and in the proper context so they can make the right decisions about relevant business relationships.

Sharing and democratizing data is mandatory in a data-driven organization. If you represent that in your company, you have to push that idea. You have to get people to understand that it is about spreading that truth everywhere. Otherwise, you are just going to be a data management silo on your own.

***

Look at your business, recognize how data is being used or managed, and map them to these 8 'Ates. These are very assessable use cases and ideas that business stakeholders can understand. I challenge you to find data that isn't used to relate, validate, integrate, aggregate, interoperate, evaluate, communicate, or circulate. A successful organization will discover these 8 'Ates in combinations across their most common and essential business processes.

Selling Your Data Story

Tips on creating a compelling narrative

Here is a story that combines my love for data and storytelling.

Long before the Gartner Data & Analytics Conference's current incarnation, it was two separate events: The

Enterprise Information Management Summit (originally called the MDM Summit) and the Business Intelligence & Analytics Summit. They were scheduled in the same location and intentionally overlapped by a few days. Each Summit had separate agendas, attendees, and exhibitors. As you might imagine, the EIM show had considerably fewer people than BI&A. I also think BI&A had better food!

One year, the EIM show was located in the basement level of the event hotel, and BI&A was on the upper level in the grand ballroom. Typical. Although EIM had a general session with a perfectly suitable speaker who was going to talk about perfectly reasonable data management use cases, the BI&A show had a keynote address on leadership and storytelling from Francis Ford Coppola.

Yes, *the* Francis Ford Coppola! One of the most important movie makers and storytellers in the history of telling stories. I have lost count of how many times I have seen *The Godfather*. There was no way I was going to miss his talk.

Armed with my EIM badge and a defiant attitude, I made my way up the basement escalators to the Emperor's Level. I marched past the attendant at the Augustus Ballroom door. I managed to get a seat in the 10th row, getting very close to the stage.

I looked enviously at the thousands of BI&A attendees tightly packed in the ballroom (versus the hundreds I knew were at the EIM Summit in the basement). I was tempted to stand up and yell, "Business intelligence doesn't work without proper data management. You are nothing without those people downstairs!" But I didn't want to blow my cover.

Coppola shared beautiful stories about making movies, the struggles of financing his cinematic dreams, and anecdotes about working with Marlon Brando. He spoke of the five generations of his movie-making family. The Coppolas have been working in Hollywood since its inception. Inspirational is an understatement. I was certifiably star struck.

The Gartner moderator opened up the floor for questions, and I had one ready. Someone in the first row asked the first question. Then the person next to them asked the second question. When the person next to *them* asked the third question, I knew the fix was in. Gartner had already decided who would ask questions. I was not deterred.

Because I was so close to the stage, I caught Coppola's eye. He nodded at me. When it came to the fourth question, he called on me.

Coppola: *So, who wants to talk about blockchain?* [laughter]. *Not that I know anything about that.* [pointing at me] *Now, what is your question?*

I stood up in front of thousands, and since they did not hand me the microphone, I drew upon my college acting training and filled the room with my voice. My face was ten feet tall on the monitor. The Gartner people in the front row were glaring at me. Cover blown! But I had my moment.

Me: *No, I don't want to talk about blockchain [laughter], but I want to ask you about stories.*

Coppola: *Good. I prefer that topic.*

Me: *Before I do, you mentioned your five generations in the movies. I want to thank you from three generations of my family who have enjoyed and been inspired by your storytelling.*

Coppola: *Thank you.*

Me: *Your ability to tell stories is so important to me that I once had a boss who, when I found out he had never seen* The Godfather, *I never felt the same way about him again.* [laughter]

When you look at a story, how do you know it's great?

Coppola: *I don't know. I suppose at night, when I am rolling around, it's all I can think about. It's like casting. You meet an actor or actress, and they just stick with you. I think my brain is like that. Like a record that plays and then it skips. It keeps repeating the same thing. It's like that with a person or a story or an idea. It just seems not to go away. I am a big believer in trusting yourself and your instinct. And your subconscious or whatever level of consciousness you have.*

Whenever I need to write something, whatever it is, I just write it any old way. And then I put it away. Then a few days later, I take it, and I know better how to rewrite it. That's because you are working on it, even when you are sleeping. It's like it is in the oven, it's cooking, and when you take it out, it's more developed. And that could be the concept for a company or a movie—same thing.

But what I have found is the great stories stick with you. They grow on you. You read them, and they keep coming back to you, calling you. Much of it is instinct. There are no rules. It is not like data, I suppose. Nothing hard and fast. You just...know.

Was I hoping for a magic secret? Yes! Was I disappointed? Absolutely not. Validation from a master storyteller.

Set your expectations based on Coppola experience. There is no magic formula for a good story. There is some science, but it is mostly art. You can have all the technique in the world, and you can take every bit of advice I have given, and it still might not fly. So, work on it. Find the compelling points and the hooks. Let it sit with you. Put it away and look at it again later. And when you get it, you'll just know.

A crash course in selling

Great storytelling has an engaging plot, vibrant imagery, and relatable characters. Classic stories have a struggle, a journey, and enlightenment towards a better way. Data storytelling needs to include the same elements told with passion and enthusiasm.

You may be wondering, what type of story is it? An epic adventure? A sci-fi fantasy? Perhaps a thriller? No, none of the above. Unlike Coppola's epics, *your* Data Story is a PITCH. It is the type of story that must drive action. You must secure a commitment that leads to further action. That action could be to increase funding, secure additional resources, deepen stakeholder involvement, or identify data ownership. Regardless, it must ask for some form of commitment. If you want to drive action in a business setting, then you need to *sell*. Your objective is to gain a commitment from your audience. All pitches end with a call to action. What action do you want from the business? In many cases, you are taking your executive audience from thinking, *"I have no idea what you're talking about"* and bringing them to the point where they exclaim, *"How do we live without this*?"

This is not a sales training book. I am not suggesting you go and take a lot of sales training, but the soft skills in sales are extremely valuable.

I have been in sales my entire career and am fourth generation sales. My father was a salesman. My grandfathers were salesmen. At the turn of the 1900s, my great grandfather was one of the first Rabbis in Texas. That was selling!

I see selling as a force for good. My father gave me a poster that has been on the wall of every office I have ever worked in. It says: *A terrible thing happens if nobody sells—NOTHING!* Bad salespeople, just like bad anything else, can sully the reputation of a craft. Selling is indeed *the oldest profession*. I know some believe something else is "the oldest profession," but hey, isn't that just selling?

As a young door-to-door salesperson, I learned that every pitch has four steps. They are based on the work of Elias St. Elmo Lewis, a pioneering advocate for the use and value of advertising in the early 1900s, These four phases that people go through when making a decision, are more formally known as the AIDA model: Attention, Interest, Desire, and Action.

- Grab Attention
- Develop Interest
- Nurture Desire
- Secure Action

You must grab somebody's *attention*, develop their *interest*, nurture their *desire*, and finally, secure their commitment to take *action*. You cannot start at the end. Your audience is not going to commit to something they do not desire. They are not going to desire it if they do not have an interest. They are not going to be interested if it never attracted their attention. We do not have to go too deep into the psychology but be aware of the cognitive process.

Conversely, if you grab the attention of your audience, they will want to know more. If their interest grows, it can develop into desire. When that desire increases, the commitment to action becomes a natural next step. These phases can happen after six months of meetings or in one minute in the elevator with your CEO. But whether you realize it or not, every request for a commitment goes through these four phases: *attention, interest, desire, action.*

Telling stories to executives

Executives may require one-on-one sessions. Make sure you cover the same topics as all the other sessions but summarize them at an executive level. If your C-level executives have chiefs of staff or other support functions, make sure you take them through the content as well. Seek their guidance on how best to format and deliver your message. You may run into some office politics, such as making sure your boss approves, and their boss and *their* boss. Of course, it depends on the personality and dynamics of your leadership. But most leaders want to hear about all areas of their business.

Once executives buy-in, then getting the help of the rest of the organization should be easier. C-Level approval gives the rest of an organization "permission to believe." You won't have to spend as much time convincing others. For tips on how to create that message, please see the section on *Illuminating Your Business Vision*.

Be ready for interruptions. C-Level executives are quick to grasp concepts—they are thinking of wide-reaching ramifications. Because of their broad field of view, they may see possibilities that you do not. And yes, they can make connections you can not. Be ready to answer their questions in the moment, especially if it is a one-on-one or small meeting. Give them an abbreviated answer if necessary, to keep your flow going. The worst thing you can do is say, "I am going to cover that later." There might not be a later.

Know how much time you have and stick to it. If executives want a meeting to go on longer, it will. But don't expect to get more time. Make sure your content would only take up about half of the scheduled meeting. You will want questions and some back and forth.

Prepare for success. Sometimes an executive leader will suddenly ask what you want next. Be ready for that. Your goal is to gain a commitment. Your objective is not *to get through all your slides*

A little story about CEOs—I have had exposure to more than my share of CEOs, and I always love talking with them. They are smart, aware, and quick to respond. While I was at Nielsen, I had the genuine honor of working directly with our CEO at the time, Dave Calhoun. He is a world-class leader. He was a top protégé of Jack Welsh while at General Electric and is now CEO of Boeing. So, this guy has done and seen it all. I was explaining a concept to him, and he suddenly said, "OK, Scott, what is the *one* thing I can do for you?" I was uncharacteristically tongue-tied and not at all ready for a corporate genie to grant my wish. I mumbled something like, "Wow, let me think about it." That was the wrong answer.

I wasn't ready for success. I vowed I would be next time—if there were ever a next time. I worked with my team to come up with a short, concise answer. As luck would have it, months later, Calhoun asked me the same thing "OK, Scott, what is the *one* thing I can do for you?" I had my answer ready. Your leader's style might be different but think of that story. Be ready for success. Have that *one* thing you need in your mind. Turn it around and offer it up. Your closing can be, "Here is the *one* thing I need from you." Don't make it five or twelve. Keep it simple. Leaders appreciate crisp delivery. It is the best way to get invited back.

Persistence is key

Every story doesn't land. Just be aware there is as much art in this approach as science. There are many factors in decisions that you will have no control over. You may not even know they exist. Emotions, other priorities, company politics, and competing interests factor into the objections you get if you are unable to secure a commitment. Keep at it. Your data management ideas will help your company. Persistence is key.

One last thing about selling

Many people pitch beyond the point of effectiveness. Once you get an agreement from your audience, you need to move forward. Do not add extra anecdotes and elaborate on concepts they have already acknowledged. You can blow the deal. I learned this first-hand early in my career. I had just closed a buyer who had given me a commitment. In my excitement, I said, "and it will be just like last year!"

The buyer said, "Really? I didn't like it last year. I am going to have to reconsider." I lost the sale in an instant. I shared this story with my father, whom I was working for at the time. He said, "Son, you have learned one of the most important lessons in sales: When you get the YES, shut up." So, when you get the YES, shut up.

That was my crash course in selling.

How not to start your data story

When you are in front of senior leadership, the opening of your presentation is critically important. It may be the only moment you get an uninterrupted portion of time. A creative and robust introduction is crucial to capture their attention. Most data management stories I have heard, however, start poorly. They often begin with something like:

- *We need better data quality* (Correct, but not a compelling hook)
- *There is more data now than ever before* (Is that really news?)
- *Data is the new oil* (No, it is neither)

False start 1 – Data quality doesn't make a good story

This may sound like heresy: data quality is not a compelling storyline. Sure, it is essential. Yes, you must have it. An objective of this book, however, is to help you *sell in* your data management program. Leaning in too hard on the quality angle doesn't work.

Without question, data needs to be accurate and actionable to provide value to any enterprise. The "need for high-quality data" has been the dominant rallying cry from data practitioners for decades. Tom Redman, The Data Doc and a world-renown, highly-respected expert on data quality, recently referenced a *Sloan Management Review* piece he wrote, stating, "our ultimate goal has been to improve data and information quality by orders of magnitude." The original article, published in 1995, reads like it was written yesterday. That's the problem.

These messages and lessons have been the same forever. There have been data quality, data hygiene, data cleanliness problems since there was data. Data and technology leaders have complained about them for eons. There are plenty of good books written by very accomplished data professionals about the importance of data quality. Years later, we use the same headlines. "Data Quality is super important." I haven't seen a rush of support from enterprise business leaders. Have you? Not saying quality isn't essential and valuable, but in terms of gaining leadership support, the harsh truth is that this approach simply hasn't worked. If data quality were a successful way to pitch for senior-level engagement, it would have worked by now. If it did, why are enterprises still suffering from fundamental data quality issues? If that tact is so successful, why are we (and you) still in the same mess? Because it does not capture anyone's imagination.

The concept of "high-quality data" does not inspire business leadership. Data quality can sound like a clerical back-office topic. It looks like a chore. And when you talk about it, sometimes emotion comes out, and you sound like you are whining. Sorry, someone has to tell you that.

Quality is an emotional, subjective, intangible word. Quality evokes soft-focus imagery of hand-crafted products and a Ricardo Mandelbaum-like voiceover cooing about "fine Corinthian leather." Although data quality metrics are essential and extremely valid within data departments, senior business leaders do not care about data quality. They care about the results.

Data quality, as a primary talking point, doesn't directly lead to business support. If you state your objective as "improving data quality," then you will immediately be asked, "why should I care?" "Well," you might reply, "then we can transform our customer experience, then we can increase throughput, then we can reduce our error rate, then we can solidify our reliability standards." By your admission, data quality is simply an enabler—a means to a greater end. Reframe it with that perspective. State your objective in the form of a business initiative:

> *We need to reduce our shipment error rate, and that will require more robust data governance for our foundational data.*

Sounds better already.

Data quality is not the destination. Although few CEOs care about data quality, all of them are passionate about customers and business relationships, as well as the satisfaction engendered from products, brands, services, and offerings. CEOs will agree that improving customer experience is mission-critical but may not understand and articulate how that connects to data quality. Instead, arm your leaders with a clear value statement linking data quality to the core efforts of the enterprise. Every enterprise system needs to leverage data. The ROI and business rationale for CRM, CDP, FinTech, MarTech, AI, BI, and ML depend on the strength of the data within those systems and processes.

If I had a minute with a CEO trying to pitch them your data quality program, I wouldn't whine about data quality. Here's how I would approach it:

We don't have a standard definition and a common structure for our customer data, and you just wrote in the annual report that we want to be 'better partners with our customers.' That we want to have 'Customer 360.' That's what our head of marketing is talking about, and we don't have the data to back it up! Let me show you why.

That sounds different to me, more strategic, more long-term, more foundational, than "our data quality sucks." There is not a CEO who thinks that they should have better data quality for the sake of better data quality. As data leaders, we have to change the conversation. With all respect to the data quality experts out there, your work is essential, but your old pitch essentially isn't working.

False start 2 – There is more data now than ever before

Last year more data was created than all the other years combined!
There is more data now than ever before.
There is more data now than there was when you started reading this sentence!
See even more now.
And now there is even more data.

It is an indisputable fact, but who cares? Yes, there is more data now than ever before. Are these statistics relevant to your business? No. There is no news here.

Figure 15. Impressive, but is this type of approach significant anymore? Or is it an unrelatable cliché?

Making grandiose claims about the sheer volume of data does not immediately lead to a rationale for your data management program. You might think that leap is obvious, but it isn't. You are just flooding the conversation with stats that you won't even come back to during your story.

False start 3 – Data is the new oil...NOT!

Is Data the new oil? No, I say, it is neither. When you open your story with that comment, are you sure your audience knows what you mean? Don't count on it. The sheer volume, variety, and velocity of debate on this phrase should be enough to make you look elsewhere to support your story. It is time to let go of DITNO. If you agree, please skip to the next chapter. If not, read on.

The purpose of imagery in a business context is to clarify and simplify an idea to make it easier to understand. DITNO isn't a clear image. This isn't a poetry contest. We are not trying to interpret the cryptic works of James Joyce. We are trying to communicate essential business opportunities clearly and concisely.

First of all, the exact wording "data is the new oil" is a *metaphor*, not a *simile*. If you remember your high school English, a simile would be "data is *like* oil" (forget the *new* part for a moment). Suggesting data is *like* oil intuitively makes some sense. That was the intention of the first use of this phrase in 2006, by Clive Humby. Humby went on to explain that data, *like* oil, "is valuable, but if unrefined, it cannot be used." Agreed. Data is fuel for analytics. Data is the lubricant between systems. Data has a higher value when refined and used correctly.

Even though *data is like oil* isn't what most people say nowadays, there has emerged a counter-argument based on the literal interpretation of it as a simile. *Oil has a limited supply. It pollutes. Oil is used only once,* and so on. Conversely, data is *sustainable. It does not pollute. Data is reusable.* Whichever side of this interpretation you are on, you have to agree that we have already spent too much time debating it to be an effective form of communication. Intellectually stimulating? Maybe. Effective business communication? No!

There is another faction suggesting that comparing data to oil reinforces the potential value. At this writing, the commodity price of oil has hit record lows. Oil is no longer immediately associated with Beverly Hillbilly-like wealth. Again, too much time to explain, too much variance in interpretation.

Doug Laney posted a deadly direct takedown of the literal interpretation of this erroneous comparison:

Data has economic properties that enable it to be leveraged in ways other assets cannot—especially oil, to which it often is erroneously compared. Data can be used simultaneously for multiple purposes. It is what economists call a non-rivalrous, non-depleting, and regenerative asset. When you consume data, it doesn't get used up, and when you do use data, it often generates yet more data.

Although Humby uttered that infamous phrase in 2006, DITNO had a recent resurgence through a consistent misinterpretation of *The Economist* article published in 2017 with the attention-grabbing headline: *The World's Most Valuable Resource Is No Longer Oil, But Data.* The article graphic has made its way into many industry presentations, webinars, and LinkedIn posts about the positive and valuable potential of data.

Figure 16 This often-used graphic does not make a positive statement about data, so don't use it.

Breaking news: This is not a positive article about data. How can you tell? Start by just reading the subhead: *The data economy demands a new approach to antitrust rules.* If that doesn't convince you, then read a little bit further, only as far as the first sentence of the article:

A new commodity spawns a lucrative, fast-growing industry, prompting <u>antitrust regulators to step in to restrain those who control its flow</u>. A century ago, the resource in question was oil. Now similar concerns are being raised by the giants that deal in data, the oil of the digital era.

This is a negative article about data. This is negative imagery for data. It suggests that there should be further regulation on Facebook, Amazon, Google, and other major digital platforms controlling data distribution and flow. Regardless of your feelings about that topic, do you still think this illustration supports your need for data management? Does this article help your rationale on the positive potential of data in your organization? At a conference, I had the opportunity to speak with Ryan Avent, the reporter who wrote this article.

"This is not a positive article about data. Is it?" I asked.

"No," he said, "it's not."

"But it's taken a life of its own, hasn't it?" I said.

"I know," he smiled.

He was thrilled. It is his story. He wants it everywhere. It spawned a further cycle of "data is the new…" fill in the blank. Data is the new gold, the new currency, the new electricity, the new black, the new bacon, even the new tofu. Does any of this help you tell your data story? No, it does not. It might be a fun parlor game. It undoubtedly gets many of us animated about the topic. But if you intend to gain support from those who do not understand data, this article is only going to scare them off.

Finally, data is not *new*. There was data before computers. There was data before electricity. One example is the *Domesday Book*—pronounced *doomsday*. It was compiled in 1089 by William the Conqueror after the Norman Conquests. (They had finally dug themselves out of their Y1K problem). The *Domesday Book* is a comprehensive tally of all people and their belongings in ancient England. Is that structured foundational data? Yes, it is.

So, data is not new. It is not oil. It is not the *new* oil. In some cases, if you must, data is *like* oil. Just leave it at that. Keep in mind, however, that ambiguity in an executive setting is not your friend.

****

Please avoid all three of these unimaginative clichés. Everyone else is saying the same thing. Each of these will make your audience impatient for you to get to the point:

why, specifically, is data management important to the business?

Some analogies that work

You may need to try different types of analogies and imagery to capture your audience's attention. Food analogies are particularly impactful. To illustrate how data is crucial to business processes, you can use the relationship between *ingredients, recipes,* and *cooks. Cooks* (the analytics team) follow *recipes* (methodologies) that require *ingredients* (data). The better the *ingredients,* the better the *meal* (business results).

Currency is also a useful analogy for the value and transferability of data. Data often becomes the *currency* between parties. *Fuel* and *electricity* are strong, reliable analogies for how data powers other activities (but not, as I mention above, as a flowery oil metaphor).

Systems	Data
Software	Content
Car	Gas
Kitchen	Food
Plumbing	Water

Figure 17 Simple analogies can help business stakeholders understand the role of data vs. systems.

Like a *clean water reservoir* servicing a community, your data management program guards, protects, and values your data content.

In his book, *The Data Garden and Other Data Allegories*, Paul Daniel Jones offers up different creative constructs to describe how data works. He suggests a titular *garden* analogy, along with a *hospital, driving school,* and others. If you are searching for ways to spark your imagination, take a look at his work.

Add some sizzle to your steak

Your narrative must effectively balance two aspects—it should be a compelling story, but it must also be technically accurate. It needs to have this balance between the *why* and the *how*. Although I focus exclusively on the *why*, I assume all of you know *how* you will execute. If you think about it metaphorically, it is that balance between the sizzle and the steak. Sizzle alone is noise. Conversely, no one wants cold steak.

You may be wondering about me suddenly bringing up the *how* part of the story. Well, if your leadership says YES, then you will need to make good on your promises. Be ready for the YES. The sizzle part of the story is all about the head-in-the-clouds imagery. You are looking to engender audience empathy, sound cool, and be inspiring.

Technical accuracy is your feet-on-the-ground approach. It details the way you will be getting it done. That may come in the form of a high-level plan, technical architecture, process flow, whatever works in your context. It has to make sense. It has to be practical. It is about the execution.

Remember, there needs to be a balance between evangelism and execution. If you over-emphasize one over the other, then you are in trouble. If it is boring techno-babble or lists of requirements, you will lose your audience. If you go too hard on the buzzy marketing spin, no one may believe you.

Figure 18 It is essential to create a balance between evangelism and execution.

CHAPTER 6

Building Your Data Story

Aligning data management with the strategic intentions of your enterprise

Now it is time to build your own data management story. To win over Business Stakeholders, data management leaders must create a compelling narrative that builds urgency, reinvigorates enthusiasm, and aligns with the strategic intentions of the enterprise. As stated, if business stakeholders do not understand and agree on the *WHY*, they will have no interest in the *HOW*. There are multiple reasons why data management programs may fail, yet an overwhelming majority suffer from an inability to demonstrate and communicate business alignment. To help solve your story problem, you need to work on what I refer to as The 3Vs of Data Management Storytelling—Vocabulary, Voice, and Vision.

This section should help you formalize and organize your narrative. You can utilize the 3Vs framework to illustrate data management's strategic importance to the broader business stakeholder community. It will allow you to be more deliberate and eventually more declarative about WHY data management is essential. Your data management narrative should effectively convey a balance between *an ability to execute* rooted in technical reality and *the alignment of vision* supported with compelling storytelling.

You may want to think of it as an internal marketing campaign and look for ways to brand your initiative. At its essence, this is a communication challenge. The bigger the company, the more you may need to fight for attention. And you will be competing against some excellent storytellers in sales, marketing, and other areas of your enterprise.

As you begin, answer these questions to approach this as an internal campaign:

- Who is your target audience? C-Level, Business Stakeholders, and data management personnel.

- What behavior and perceptions need to be changed? *This topic is not important. We have other priorities. Not my area—It's an IT thing.*

- What commitments and actions do you require? More significant support, improved compliance, on-going funding.

Leveraging the 3Vs of data management storytelling

Constructing a narrative for your data management story is not a trivial undertaking you can leave until the last minute. Getting your group organized around a common theme and approach will do wonders to evangelize the need for the work you and your team do. But it is *work*. I do not expect you to write the next *Harry Potter* series, but just like J. K. Rowling, you need to shape your narrative around specific themes. To help, here are three areas that need attention: The words you use, the way you say them, and what they will mean. Many organizations suffer from a lack of business support because:

- The **Vocabulary** is confusing
- The **Voice** is discordant
- The **Vision** is blurred

When communicating to executive leadership and business stakeholders, skip the technical details, the feature/functionality, or the reference architecture and focus on:

- Establishing an accessible **Vocabulary**
- Harmonizing to a common **Voice**
- Illuminating the business **Vision**

Establish an accessible vocabulary

The words we use are important. To speak to the business, you must use the vocabulary of your business. To be convincing, you must go well beyond the legacy lexicon of the enterprise data management space. See my section about over-emphasizing "data quality." Again, I believe data quality is a critical aspect of data management, but it does not make for a compelling storyline.

Similarly, concepts such as "cleansing" or "freshness" may be necessary, but they are hardly holistic and rarely strategic. Most "data hygiene" exercises are ad-hoc, campaign-based projects isolated to a siloed use case. In business discussions, replace vague terms, such as "quality, cleansing, freshness and hygiene" with definitive words like "structure, standards, coverage, and interoperability."

Begin with the terminology and nomenclature used in your enterprise and industry vertical. Much of this is probably already captured in your business glossary. Capture the terms for all your business relationships and brand offerings. Ask your business associates to explain things in their language. Start with the most granular level of your relationships. As an example, many industries refer to *customers* as their primary relationship. Law firms and advertising agencies, however, call them *clients*. Packaged goods manufacturers refer to their retail partners as *customers* and their end-users as *consumers*. A hospital would never refer to a *patient* as a *customer*.

The purpose of this terminology is to establish a common language for your organization. If you are a global company, your vocabulary must resonate globally, sometimes across multiple cultures. The terms you use should map directly to your master data domains and represent most of your data's subject areas.

Additionally, establish a consistent vocabulary for the hierarchy levels, segmentations, and market geographies. These are essential piece parts of your business. You will notice they correlate to the 4Cs described above (review that section for additional terminology). Leverage the standard vocabulary in your industry vertical. There are undoubtedly trade associations, standards organizations, and other governing bodies in your industry. Many have industry glossaries you can leverage to immediately establish credibility for your story.

I recently saw a job posting for a master data manager at a global pharmaceutical company. The posting included a mother lode of vocabulary for this organization as well as its industry at large. The different master data domains had generally-recognizable entity types such as *patients, payers, employees, contracts, vendors, sites, and products* along with very specific industry terminology: *omics, compounds, diseases, CROs, trials, KOLs, HCPs, EMR, EHR, and patient journeys.*

Example of a Pharmaceutical Company's Vocabulary
Commonly recognized terms
Patients, Payers, Employees, Contracts, Vendors, Sites, And Products
Industry-specific nomenclature
Omics, Compounds, Diseases, Trials, CROs, KOLs, HCPs, EMR, EHR

Figure 19 A vocabulary will combine widely recognized terms and the nomenclature of the specific industry vertical.

Avoid technical jargon and process descriptions. Invariably you will need to use some form of acronyms—often referred to as TLAs. (TLA is a three-letter acronym for Three-Letter Acronym. Talk about meta!) Explain any TLAs to ensure your audience understands them. The same three letters can mean entirely different things to different people in the same meeting.

Here is a little data story to illustrate my point. A marketing executive and a data scientist had a status call with their CEO.

"We need SQL," said the data scientist.

"We need SQL," said the Marketing Exec.

"Yes, we need another one!" said the CEO.

Everyone left the meeting, confused.

While you might know that SQL stands for *structured query language*, it also stands for *sales qualified lead* in marketing. This confused CEO thought they heard the word "sequel."

There are many overused (i.e., popular) terms in the data management space that may not help you make your point. We say "golden record" all the time. Your CEO might think, "golden? Well, that sounds expensive!"

Other technology categories have diluted phrases like "single version of the truth." A *single version of truth* (SVOT) seems to benefit nearly every type of data consolidation application. Even analytics platforms and cloud-storage vendors bandy about this phrase. The problem it presents is that when you say SVOT, people will not always know what you mean.

Answer these questions to avoid tactical, technical terminology:

- What is the terminology and nomenclature used in your enterprise and industry vertical?

- What is the most granular business relationship? (Customer, account, client, store, door, consumer, citizen, or patient?)

- How do you refer to your products, brands, and offerings?

- What terms do you use to describe hierarchy relationships, customer segmentation, and market geographies? (Remember the 4Cs of Data Structure.)

- What is your data management program called? Does that resonate and build excitement with the business stakeholders, or is it just the software platform's name?

Naming your data management program

If you think of your data program as an internal brand, it will need a name. You want to capture the spirit of what you are doing. Catchy acronyms can often reinforce the scope and importance of the project. Many people use mythical and heroic terms. PEGASUS is a good one— **P**roviding **E**nterprise **G**overnance **A**nd **S**tewardship **U**ser **S**ervices. A trendy name for the *second* attempt at a data management program is *Phoenix* because the first one burned down!

Frank Cerwin of Data Mastery Inc. has an excellent tip about naming your program. "Never use the name of the software vendor," advises Cerwin. "The software might change. Or you may merge with another company, and their software might replace yours." As he suggests, find a name that reflects your internal brand, not the brand of your vendor.

Simplicity always reigns in naming. Don't get too cute, and don't *over*-name. You will not need an internal brand for everything. There is a balance. Remember, you are trying to support existing activity and help organize and unify your business. Adding too much can sometimes be worse than not enough.

Harmonize to a common voice

The Voice is the prevailing tenor and tone of your narrative. Think about how you sound to your audience. If every team member tells the same story in different ways, it will be a confusing and conflicting mess. Solidify your messaging—like any pitch, and it has to be memorable.

The bigger the organization, the simpler your message needs to be. You have to find ways to make your influence scale. Don't add a lot of qualifiers and nuances. If you think you always have to be in the room to explain your message, then it is too complicated.

In media, they talk about reach and frequency. The reach is the number of people who are exposed to your message. Frequency means reinforcing the same, consistent, sometimes singular message. You need to work on both. To increase reach, consider your range of delivery. Your audience members are different types of people with different ways of absorbing messaging. Some love the fun and exciting approach. In particular, salespeople like to hear a good pitch, appreciate humor, and want something they can easily repeat. Others, especially in finance, legal, and IT, can be very skeptical. Not saying they don't appreciate the fun side, but they will be looking for depth.

Don't count on a one-size, one-format fits-all approach. Find different ways to say the same thing while staying focused myopically on your message: formal presentations, lunch and learns, panel discussions, and internal podcasts. Videos are a must. Write a one-pager: *Why Data Management Will Help Grow, Improve, and Protect Our Business Relationships: A Call to Action.* If you cannot do that, then your message is not strong enough. This is hard work! I understand. But it isn't as hard as fixing data in your organization without any on-going support.

Look for data heroes and supporters in other parts of the organization. Find that finance person who depends on hierarchies. Locate a sales executive who closed a recent deal because they had the right data. Search for that administrator who is always explaining data in simple terms for their peers. Listen to their ideas and incorporate them into your training. Identify and track them. These supporters will expand your reach and increase your frequency. Identify your stakeholders and segment your audience. Who are your supporters and internal influencers?

Recruit internal influencers from other departments. Having supporters representing sales, marketing, finance, operations, legal, and other functional areas will significantly increase your credibility. Invite them to participate in an internal panel discussion. Have them articulate why the outputs of data management have helped their function. Why has better data made their job better? These are potent vignettes you want to capture. Depending on your corporate culture, there can be all sorts of opportunities to spotlight these individuals.

Borrow and emulate as much of your company marketing as possible. If you have a company statement or slogan, co-opt it. Make your data management brand a variant of your corporate brand. It could be as easy as replacing a few words in your company tagline with *data management*. Perhaps there is a pun or play on words that can incorporate your company's brands. Be creative.

Consider both digital and physical media. Posters, stickers, pins, hats, even some gamification. People love to earn badges and award certificates to display on-line and in offices. Show that you are building a community that understands and supports data management. Quick example: When I was at Dun & Bradstreet, I wanted to illustrate the versatility of master data as both a product on its own and an ingredient in everything we did. I did a training session using baking soda as the analogy. Baking soda can be used for baking, cleaning, and deodorizing. It is also a branded ingredient in toothpaste, household cleaner, and other products. Master data is the same type of thing. It had value on its own as well as being an ingredient in multiple products. I went a step further and created a custom label for a baking soda box. I converted the Arm & Hammer imagery to Dun & Bradstreet.

Figure 20 Look for creative analogies to explain the value of data management outputs.

We handed out the re-labeled baking soda boxes to the sales team. I put one in every refrigerator I could find in every office I visited through some guerrilla marketing. I included a sticker that said, "if you want to know why master data is like baking soda, contact Scott Taylor." Similarly, your data management program's output is like baking soda—there are many direct and indirect uses.

Create a short, standardized overview or "elevator pitch" about data management. Avoid in-depth technical explanations. Use simple business language. Create a short version of your story that you can tell crisply and succinctly. I know it is hard to boil down your messaging. It takes time to limit words and cut slides. But you must make that effort. People will always ask for more if they are interested, but you risk never making your point if you go on forever. I once had a speaking slot that was only ten minutes. My opening line was, "It has taken me 20 years to get this down to ten minutes!"

A former co-worker of mine, Kimberley Haley, has an excellent tip she called the Coco Chanel Rule:

Coco Chanel, the famous French fashion designer, once said, "Simplicity is the keynote of all true elegance." This is just as applicable in a presentation. Keep the slides, data, and talking points simple, and your message will be well received. Coco Chanel also said: "before leaving the house, look in the mirror and remove one accessory." I challenge myself to see if I can remove one more slide before I consider my presentation finished.

That challenge pushes me to think more simply and refine the message and the goals even more.

Practice and edit. Get fluent in your content, and then you can work on delivery. If you were ever in a theatrical play, you memorize your lines first and then work on the acting part. Don't wait to give your presentation until it is time to perform. I know you might think it is harder to practice than actually to do it. Get in front of someone who knows the story well and make sure it works. Listen to feedback—practice in the mirror. Record yourself and listen to it. It may feel awkward at first, but you will begin to hear flaws in reasoning, holes in logic, and verbal tics. Get rid of them. I have executed thousands of presentations. I still record and listen to them. I always find ways to improve. You are your own best teacher.

Create a collection of business success stories from collaborative partners in sales, marketing, finance, analytics, and operations. Identify and clearly articulate the specific pain points that data management can relieve. Focus on results and benefits instead of process steps and features. Tie these together with the common motif of data management as an enabler. Share these stories regularly across your stakeholder community.

Formalize an internal communication plan. A company newsletter or blog is a great way to increase awareness and engagement. I have seen plenty of examples of internal data management newsletters. Get something posted in your internal company communications vehicles. People in your corporate communications department are always looking for stories to share. Ask for a regular column and highlight the "data management hero of the month."

Establish an education and training schedule through regular meetings or webinars. Resist making this a rote, boring training course. Data management training is a requirement too, but if you don't bring excitement and enthusiasm to the topic, then your audience will find this experience a chore. Remember, most people think data is boring. You have a passion for the subject—you need to share it.

Finally, ensure your direct and extended team share a common viewpoint and position on the value of data management. Harmonize your voice.

Illuminate the business vision

The Vision of your data management program must directly support the vision of your company. *All investments in data management should enable the strategic intentions of your enterprise.* If your data strategy isn't the same as your business strategy, then it, and maybe both, will fail. In today's business climate, the pressure is more intense, and the stakes are much higher. You need to embody that urgency with your leadership. You need to keep a message going that your company's goals may not materialize if you don't have the data to back them up.

Part of the challenge is that data management, on its own, has no distinct value. It must enable other efforts. To identify the connections between data management and strategic initiatives, locate and rigorously review strategy documents presented by business leadership (i.e., investor day presentations, annual reports, employee newsletters, or other declarations of company intentions). Determine the role data management plays in those efforts centered around business growth, operational efficiency, and risk mitigation.

You will need to perform some good old-fashion due diligence on your own company. Scour your company's top priorities and find each mention of relationships (customer, vendor, supplier, client, partner, prospect, patient, consumer, citizen) and brands (product, service, offering, location, banner, property, asset). Look for any form of analytics (BI, AI, ML, DL), and you will uncover the need for the steady flow of highly structured, standardized, secure, trusted content about those entities.

I have determined that most businesses talk about needing data management without really talking about it. It is whispered between the lines of strategy statements and behind the scenes of major corporate initiatives. Many industry hot topics are raising strategic temperatures for data management:

- The foundational basis of Machine Learning is "training data", which allows us to tell machines what to do. Inconsistent, unmastered data lead to flawed programs.

- The operating theory of the Internet of Things (IoT) is a seamless connection. Everything needs to connect to everything else *when it should*. It is the "should" that is the most formidable goal to achieve.

- Digital Twins are replicas of physical assets or devices operating in a business enterprise. To successfully create and manage a digital twin requires highly-structured reliable data.

- The promise of the 4th Industrial Revolution is based on machines and devices "talking" to other machines and devices. That process is "I have to find something, determine if I can trust it, and then connect to it." The ideal response is, "I have what you need to find, you can trust me, and here's how to connect." But unfortunately, the answer is often, "I don't even understand what you're looking for," or "I think this is what you're looking for, but I'm not sure." During these connections, identity validation creates trust, and metadata structure enables integration.

- COVID-19 has thrown some companies headlong into forms of digital transformation, thereby requiring better-managed data to survive. For example, many organizations have to significantly deepen their e-commerce capabilities, requiring a fast upgrade to their product data and related content.

I do not suggest you attempt to convince leadership that improving data management is more critical than any single item already on their corporate priority list. As a solo effort, data management will never become a corporate priority. Nor should it, but here is why that is an opportunity. Having reliable data is a mandatory requirement for most, if not all, corporate priorities. Study the key business initiatives of your organization. Do those objectives have anything to do with increasing market penetration? Operational efficiency? Mitigating risk? Strengthening security? Authenticating identity? Mergers and acquisitions? Data management plays a mission-critical role in all of those.

The data management discussion can no longer be relegated to the IT domain—it should be front-and-center in a business strategy and management discussion chaired by at least one top corporate leader and board member.

For organizations that are not culturally aligned to using existing information, every system or process runs the risk of creating new data sets. Time to success is inversely proportional to the count of systems. To keep a successful implementation on track, clearly identify your stakeholders and attend to them strategically. Produce and manage an implementation roadmap that shows a steady stream of data project accomplishments. Prioritize your efforts carefully. The simple top-down approach, basing priority on expenditures or sales, can prove data management value quickly. Tackle some of your largest relationships in an early phase. Work with those partners who are willing to experiment and test.

To drive adoption, set organization-wide data standards for collection, delivery, and maintenance. Then enforce consistent compliance with internal standards. Strict and formal governance is needed: Clearly define a strategy for leveraging information and elevate the importance of data across the organization—support for data management will soon follow. Finally, trust in those who guard your data as a hard asset. If data is not valued, investments in its management will not be valued either.

Your story needs to capture the hearts and minds of your business leadership. Certainly, return-on-investment calculations and cost-per-record savings can help those trying to fund one-time cleanup efforts and tactical projects. Data management, however, needs to become a holistic enterprise program. Because everyone benefits, isolating funding can be difficult. With growing pressure on investments to produce quicker and more defined payback, many stakeholders may perceive an individual risk of supporting something for the greater good. Middle management, especially, may consider data management to be a *tax* or a *toll*. They might complain that they never see any direct benefit. Therefore, your story must prove why it helps the entire enterprise holistically.

Formalize and organize your data story by uncovering your company vision and expose the data challenges that, in many cases, are hidden in plain sight. It is your task to discover them.

A data management program goes well beyond technical requirements. It demands a strategic understanding of the business direction and marketplace dynamics. Business alignment, careful planning around business nomenclature, and agreement across the organization are paramount.

Take KNOW for an answer

It is impossible to know too much about your company. You must take *know* for an answer. Know your business language. Know your goals and problems. Know your environment and data, be fluent in your go-to-market dynamics. Know your company strategy.

Every interaction you have with members of other teams will enlighten you to the need for better data. The more you listen for these clues, the easier it will be for you to detect them. Non-data conversations around building *relationships* and growing *brands* are always data conversations behind the scenes. By understanding the strategic goals, you will find your company's Vision. Reviewing how an organization articulates value through your brand is the essence of your Voice. Collecting and unifying your company's nomenclature is the basis of your Vocabulary.

Understanding your business dynamics

Here are a set of directional questions that will help you articulate the need for strategic support of data management. I use these as part of my due diligence process to help companies understand their data management story. You may not need to answer all of them, but this should give you a good list of things to look for.

Organizational Objectives

- What are the organization's pain points that are currently high on the list of company goals?

- What are the Business Drivers that are already supported by data management?
- Do you have a well-defined business problem you are trying to solve?
- Is this a defined project?
- Is it a reengineering or a new initiative?
- Which internal organization is sponsoring your data management initiative?
- What is the working relationship between IT and the Business?
- At what level within the organization do you have executive sponsorship for this initiative?
- Does this problem have visibility, priority across multiple groups such as Sales, Marketing, Finance, and other departments and disciplines?
- Have you established any success metrics for your data management project?
- Do you have any quantifiable business case information concerning data management?
- What is your time frame to show success with this program?
- What resources and people within your company do you have access to that have been part of a data management project?
- Is there a systems integrator in place assisting you with this initiative?

Tools / Systems

- Do you have any data profiling tools, or have you done a data profile on your current data sets?
- What have you been using to match like records today? Manual or tools?
- Do you have any tools for managing enterprise metadata?
- What systems are you using for Business Intelligence / Reporting / Analysis?
- Do you have an existing enterprise-wide data dictionary?

Data and Data Quality

- What are the documented definitions of relationship types (customer, vendor, partner, prospect, consumer, citizen, patient) and brand elements (product, service, offering, variant, location, banner, ingredient, materials, parts)?
- Which system is currently considered to hold your "record of truth"?
- Have you quantified the quality of your data and the improvements you expect with data management?
- Do you know who is organizationally responsible for implementing your data governance policies?
- What metrics do you currently have to measure data accuracy and usage?

Current Implementation and Process

- Are your systems and process requirements defined? Have you engaged any vendors?
- What are the various processes that are a part of your day-to-day activities regarding master data?
- What is the record creation process for your master data?
- Do you have defined stewardship and survivorship rules?
- What sources of data create new records?
- What sources will feed into your data management environment?
- Can you also provide the "application name/function," "number of records each system," and "number of account/customer/leads creates" within each application that integrates with the data management system?
- Do you have visibility on the lifecycle of core enterprise business objects in your organization?
- Do you have any defined data lifecycle processes for your organization?
- What endpoints will benefit from the data management process?

Data Integration and Application Implementation

- What tools are you using for master data management regarding master data creation, data quality, and data integration?

- What are the touchpoints and integration to/from the data management environments?
- Are there any gaps in the current integration workflow?
- What are the improvements that you seek in the current process?
- Is there a specific language or technology stack used to build applications within your organization?

CHAPTER 7

Finding the Data Story

Here are examples of individual enterprise scenarios that all call for a data management program's strategic support. I have tried to frame these stories generically to highlight the common issues and challenges. The individual companies are less important than the emerging patterns and motifs.

While your challenges and issues may feel like they are particular to your business, rest assured many others face nearly identical conditions. As you read through these, you will undoubtedly find similarities to your situation. You may feel special, but you are not unique.

Where possible, we also want to find clues for all the 3Vs. What is the Vocabulary, Voice, and Vision of these companies? Other frameworks I have introduced in this book are also applicable. To codify the structure for relationship and brand data, use the 4Cs. To organize the ways a company will use data try mapping activities to the 8 'Ates. I am not suggesting you need to explain my frameworks to your target audience but simply use them to guide your preparation and creation process. They can help you organize your thinking and ensure you have not missed any critical elements of your story.

Example 1 – Generic enterprises

At a typical global enterprise, you are going to find some classic data management challenges. For example, there is always a need for global reporting for the most important relationships and brands. This reporting needs to align with regional activity. That stress already causes consternation between local and global needs to manage customer and brand hierarchies across regions. You need a global standard for the critical domains while maintaining regional system integrity. If you draw this out as the example shows below, you may have different regions supported by separate primary systems. Although they use the same domain name, their local customers are counted separately and defined differently.

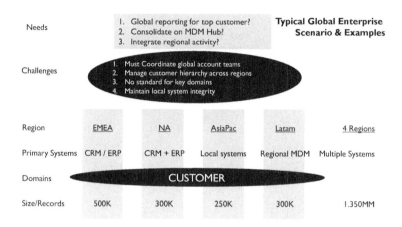

Needs	1. Global reporting for top customer? 2. Consolidate on MDM Hub? 3. Integrate regional activity?				**Typical Global Enterprise Scenario & Examples**
Challenges	1. Must Coordinate global account teams 2. Manage customer hierarchy across regions 3. No standard for key domains 4. Maintain local system integrity				
Region	EMEA	NA	AsiaPac	Latam	4 Regions
Primary Systems	CRM / ERP	CRM + ERP	Local systems	Regional MDM	Multiple Systems
Domains	CUSTOMER				
Size/Records	500K	300K	250K	300K	1.350MM

Figure 21 A whiteboard example of a typical global enterprise with regional silos.

Flipping this idea organizationally, we can just look at it from the perspective of executive personas. Here we see the departments they lead and the primary system that facilitates their siloed activity.

For example, the sales department is represented by the Chief Sales Officer (CSO), whose primary system is a Customer Relationship Management (CRM) tool. The Chief Marketing Officer (CMO), however, is using a Customer Data Platform (CDP) targeting system to manage audience information. The Chief Operating Officer (COO), as the operations lead, manages the Enterprise Resource Planning (ERP) system for the fulfillment of products. Finance, of course, uses its FinTech applications to manage compliance and billing. At the beginning of the supply chain, the CPO uses a procurement system for purchasing ingredients and supplies from particular vendors. Add onto this even more external sources from agencies, syndicated research firms, and other partners managed by the Chief Data Officer (CDO). You begin to see a rather complicated yet classic scenario where silos, systems, and departments have no common standards.

C-Level Needs Initiatives GTM			CEO Top customer teams Expansion through M&A Direct & Distributors			Typical Local Enterprise Scenario & Examples
Challenges			Siloed systems and departments / multiple regions / no common standards			
Department	Sales	Marketing	Operations	Procurement	Finance	Data
Persona	CSO	CMO	COO	CPO	CFO	CDO
Example System	CRM	CDP	ERP	Supply	FINTECH	More Sources Agencies Markets Media spend
Use case	Customer create	Targeting	Fulfillment	Purchasing	Compliance	Syndicated Research
Example Sources	Field	Web forms	Invoice	Orders	Billing	Sales tracking Customer Insight
Domains	CUSTOMER	PROSPECT	CUSTOMER	VENDOR	CUSTOMER	Partners Distributors
Standardized data integrated into systems and workflows						

Figure 22 A whiteboard example of a typical enterprise with departmental and persona-based silos.

Part of the point of this repetitive exercise is to help you identify patterns. What begins to emerge is something you can draw consistently: *Problems represent columns and rows depict solutions*. Vertical silos integrate across the horizontal.

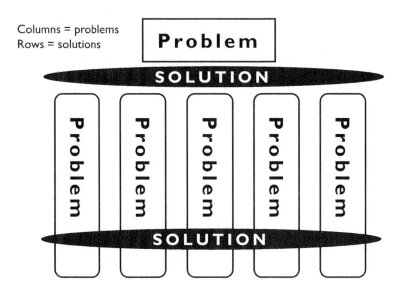

Figure 23 Draw problems as columns and solutions as rows.

Example 2 – Fortune 200 company investor day presentation

Remember, a data management effort must *enable the strategic intentions of your enterprise.* If you are part of a public company, there is no easier way to discover those intentions than to listen to what your leaders say. In this case, we will look at some highlights of the investor day presentation publicly presented by the senior leadership of a Fortune 200 company. In this investor day presentation, business leadership shared its direction, objectives, and strategy through a high-level plan and statement:

We aspire to be the premier partner of choice for our customers, suppliers, and shareholders. Our company does business in over 90 countries with over 100,000 customers and 800 suppliers. Our strategic framework is built on customer engagement, enterprise effectiveness, and brand management. We have a commitment to standard platforms that help us differentiate our customer experience and manage local productivity and efficiency. We have a constant mantra—be more efficient, deliver high-quality service levels, spend less on sustaining, and deliver more innovation.

The Vision of this company is clearly stated in the first sentence. "We aspire to be the premier partner of choice for our customers, suppliers..." The executive team identified the company's primary relationships and those map directly to the master data domains of customer and supplier. The voice of the company is within the objectives *of customer engagement, enterprise effectiveness, and brand management.* Inherent in all three of those activities is the desire to grow, improve, and protect the business. Their "constant mantra… to be more efficient and deliver high-quality service levels" links directly to growth and improvement objectives. They also refer to differentiating their customer experience and focusing on *local productivity and efficiency.* These types of comments clearly show the need for technology as a way to scale and provide more value and drive innovation.

The company's vocabulary is embedded in their relationship types and brands. They have multiple operational and sales regions within their 90-country geographic footprint. There are undoubtedly all kinds of hierarchy and categorization terminology, with over one hundred thousand customers and eight hundred suppliers. This exposes the dire need for highly-structured data behind the scenes.

Having engaged with this company, I was able to look at their internal data and found some systemic data management challenges. As an example, in one region, they had 185 copies of a single customer entity. While there could be some operational justification for multiple records, this was way beyond any reasonable limit. So, through a representative data sample, you can easily challenge the practicality of their stated vision. You can imagine how many bad decisions would be made off a file containing 185 copies of the same record. We go quickly from this aspirational vision to be *the premier partner of choice* in the relationships to the data reality of having hundreds of duplicates for major customers within major markets.

Example 3 – Global financial services company – Annual report

An annual report is another excellent source to find the strategic intentions of a given enterprise. In the next example, we look at a large financial services organization and identify its data story from its annual report. In this annual report, they mention the market dynamics and trends affecting their category and the aspirations of their enterprise:

- Quickly emerging as a critical advisor on the digitization of business
- Seeking new technology-driven solutions
- The need for innovative solutions to create more secure and rewarding futures
- The dynamic and shifting environment places a premium on trusted consulting advice and expertise
- Predictive insights derived from machine learning
- Achieve competitive advantages through the power of data
- In the last decade, over 100 acquisitions and investments that have made us stronger
- Disruption and innovation in distribution platforms and technologies

These statements would suggest that this company wants to apply technology to every part of its business to help grow, improve, and protect the value it delivers to its relationships through its brands. Data management is an enabler for every one of these objectives. Note that the *decade of over 100 acquisitions and investments* suggests an incredible number of disparate systems and a potential lack of an internal standard.

Further research showed that many of their documented internal objectives and projects map directly to The 8' Ates:

1. **Relate.** To become one of the very best companies, not merely in our industry segments, but the world. To achieve this, we must be relevant to clients.

2. **Validate.** Ensure clean, accurate information. Reduce compliance issues.

3. **Integrate.** Enrich company data with third party attributes.

4. **Aggregate.** Legal family tree information to secure and increase service revenue. Maximize cross-sell / Up-sell opportunities.

5. **Interoperate.** Scale operational processes internally and through self-service customer interface.

6. **Evaluate.** Enable reporting benchmarking, client revenue analytics, and more granular profitability measures.

7. **Communicate.** Map products locally and globally. Need for a common language for programs.

8. **Circulate**. Systematic approach to improve, control, and distribute core data to downstream business applications and supporting systems.

Example 4 – Global services company – Strategic presentation

A services company articulated its critical initiatives during a strategic presentation. This global enterprise identified *critical long-term capabilities* needed *to deliver and sustain the value objectives.*

1. Customer self-service
2. Dispute management
3. Contract management
4. Effective pricing
5. Billing and invoicing

This company shared its initiative to upgrade its customer care center with additional self-service functionality that would directly impact reducing call volume to customer care centers, increase overall customer experience, and create more up-sell opportunities.

They are focused on upgrading additional capabilities for:

- E-commerce
- Marketing automation
- Salesforce automation
- Configure price and quote
- Contract lifestyle management
- Incentive compensation management
- Case management
- Enterprise resource planning
- Business intelligence

The presentation was filled with terms like relationship management, buyer journey, customer experience ecosystem, account hierarchy levels, and the need for more in-depth customer insight.

Their customer success department wanted integrated activity from customer service, risk management, customer engagement, customer insight and intelligence, and the renewal process.

Every one of these capabilities touches a varied set of this company's relationships and supports its entire brand portfolio. All of them require a data management program. None of them stated the declarative need for quality data, data management, MDM, reference data, master data, or metadata. Yet, a perceptive data leader will know and must link all of these initiatives to the successful output of their data management program.

In this case, the data leaders did identify a data quality root cause coming from inflexible billing arrangements, inadequate manual company matching rules, no standard company hierarchy, and agreements hardwired to particular relationships, which resulted in duplicate contracts, duplicate companies, and duplicate agreements. Their data management approach included better matching, more attention to global hierarchies, sourcing third-party data for value-added enrichment, and direct integration with their sales and marketing tools. They also recommended an integrated *search before create* process to stop duplicates before they happened.

Example 5 – Consumer goods company – Various inputs

This example comes from a casual discussion I had with a data leader at an industry conference. I then reviewed their website and company report. This consumer goods company produces *a family of iconic brands available in more than 70 countries.* The following megatrends, as they put it, were shaping their business:

- They were strengthening their omnichannel customer experience and looking at a strong mix of distribution channels.

- They employed a wide variety of local suppliers and vendors for the materials needed to produce their products.

- They sought to strengthen partnerships and increase efficiency by building a unified platform with global capabilities that optimized the global supply chain.

- They wanted to follow an entity from a lead to a prospect to a customer. This process touched multiple systems and different departments.

- Their overriding product philosophy was to *get it right the first time*. But that same philosophical outlook did not apply to their data.

They faced a tremendous number of challenges. They had fifteen ERP systems as well as multiple CRM and other systems serving different markets and different brands. They had multi-country customers with no consistent way to connect to the local legal entities—each with a different local tax ID.

They suffered from a tremendous number of issues regarding data governance. Their files were littered with *incorrect countries of origin, wrong primary contact points incorrect, and inconsistent global hierarchies.* The organization lacked any standard view of customers or suppliers. Because this was an iconic brand with a long, rich heritage, in some cases, they had contracts that dated back multiple decades. They were overwhelmed by the idea of creating a single ERP system but knew they needed a global perspective for customers. They were striving to validate their customer data before uploading and into the ERP. They needed multilevel hierarchies for local, global, and brand views.

By demonstrating that these separate but critical needs were all related to data management, they were able to convince business leaders to invest in a global program.

Example 6 – Consumer insight can drive the need for data management

The need for data management can lurk in a much bigger marketing initiative. I have witnessed many projects with brand owners looking for more in-depth consumer insights and innovative ways to communicate and engage with their consumer audience. The need for data management is inherent in their requests but often "hidden in plain sight." To the trained data management eye, you can find this need and work to make it more apparent to the stakeholders. Large global brands often seek and request these typical requirements. Without a strategic data management program in place, it is impossible to fulfill these requirements and operationalize these initiatives. Requirements often include:

- Globally consistent product category definitions in all countries
- Simplified industry-standard hierarchies
- Consistent categorization of owned and competitive brands
- Harmonized data across all countries, ensuring a single lens focus on business performance management
- Integration of brand and communications data
- Dashboards for measurement of brand activity with global and local views
- Display of marketing KPIs across the entire brand portfolio
- Tracking and campaign management by distribution channel
- Consolidation of core KPIs to gain a broader understanding of marketing cause and effect
- Overall brand activities through a combination of different data types

Unilever, a global manufacturer, published an excellent data management story. Their need for data management came from marketing and consumer research. Unilever makes fast-moving consumer goods in multiple categories and sells them across an enormous number of locations. They arguably have the most complicated and far-reaching distribution and go-to-market process of any company on earth. According to company figures, 2.5 billion people in 190 Countries use their 400+ brands each day. Their products range from household supplies to beverages to frozen desserts. It is impossible to deliver all their products in a single truck or a consolidated distribution method. Bar soap cannot travel with ice cream. Detergent is handled differently than chilled beverages. Their case study, published in the Harvard Business Review, titled *Building an Insights Engine*, stated that their "new source of competitive advantage is customer centricity: deeply understanding your customers' needs and fulfilling them better than anyone else." It details the effectiveness of harnessing consumer data at scale.

Working closely with IT, Unilever implemented a global marketing-information system, accessible to all marketers throughout the company, that integrates data and presents it in consistent formats. This ensures that all users, wherever they reside in the firm, see the same information in the same way, "one version of the truth."

The study outlines the operational characteristics needed to create this capability. The first one is "data synthesis." Despite the value in the other operational characteristics, this data journey started with a global requirement for data management. Unilever worked across its agency and research supplier base on establishing a standard protocol for data delivery. They mandated a common data structure for product identification, brand hierarchies, competitive categories, and consumer geographies. Note the similarity to my 4Cs of Data Structure—code, company, category, and country. Data management provided the underlying infrastructure to enable Unilever's strategic intentions.

Example 7 – A Cautionary Tale – The $400,000,000 fine for lack of Data Governance

Sometimes when data management doesn't get the strategic attention it deserves, that *becomes* the story. Citibank was fined $400 million by the US Department of Treasury for failure "to implement and maintain an enterprise-wide data governance program commensurate with the Bank's size, complexity, and risk profile."

In the formal complaint, easily found on the web, Citi is required to "develop an acceptable Data Governance Plan" that will, among other things:

- Identify all gaps between the Bank's current data governance state and the ongoing and planned corrective actions required

- Establish and ensure adherence to consistent and comprehensive data policies, procedures, and standards

- Strengthen procedures and processes for identifying, reporting, monitoring, escalating, and remediating all data quality concerns

- Strengthen procedures and processes for the continuous improvement of data quality

- Simplify and consolidate applications with common functionalities, eliminate disparate systems, and strengthen data quality controls

- Ensure consistent adoption of authoritative data sources, reference data sets, enterprise-data sets

Here we have a major global enterprise that did not take data management seriously and failed to protect its brand and data. This horrific data story is the exception that proves every one of my rules. No one wants this type of regulatory scrutiny to be the WHY in their business rationale to manage data. Let it be a cautionary data tale for your organization.

CONCLUSION

Living Happily Ever After

Data can change the nature of your business. Just look around you. The common thread in most successful companies today is their ability to harness the power of data. That is an exciting opportunity.

In today's environment, I would challenge you to find another factor that can create this sort of change. Product management? It is incredibly difficult for established organizations to develop new disruptive products. It can certainly happen, but it is a long road. Sales? It is very challenging for a large sales organization to pivot to support new business models. Marketing can position your company with new creative, but will that profoundly change the nature of your business? Perhaps. But suppose you are in the "Data Department." In that case, if you own the management of data in your organization, you have the unique opportunity to change the very nature of how your business grows, improves, and protects itself.

There is no other variable that offers this type of potential. Well-managed data is a distinct competitive advantage. Look up the whitepapers from every leading technology and management consultant. They offer plenty of research to confirm that data-driven, data-mature organizations consistently outperform their less data-savvy peers. You can be part of how your enterprise changes the way it *delivers value to your relationships through your brands at scale.*

With the tremendous growth in platforms and the concurrent explosion of data sources, enterprises and their partners cannot profitably and efficiently manage the business without a sustainable data management program. The market, relationships, and future growth prospects will continue to suffer from manual, ad-hoc, and non-integrated processes that waste resources and impede the path to implementation and efficiency. A data management program that is well planned and executed within individual companies ultimately strengthens all parts of the value chain: customers, suppliers, distributors as well as the third-party research and service providers that support them. Data management can touch and improve every transaction, plan, analysis, and budget. Conversely, organizations that lack data management likely will continue on an ever-deepening spiral of siloed, segregated, and inflexible business processes.

As a leader or potential leader in your organization, you can see that the time is now to focus your sights on instituting a data management program for the overall health and satisfaction of your business relationships. This is a business-led initiative that uses technology-based solutions to deliver on a clear data management roadmap. Data management is critical to improving existing processes that drive business today—thus, it is foundational to fulfill future business strategy and meet the challenges of continuous market evolution and disruption.

Considering the debilitating challenges inherent in maintaining redundant internal systems, negotiating the lack of data governance and standards, and managing a constantly changing marketplace, it is easy to see why data management initiatives must have a place in the strategic landscape.

Start, stop, continue

While I hope this book has helped you add some sizzle to your steak, you still need the steak. Suppose your audience loves your new story—you still have to make it a reality. Data management doesn't have the best reputation. Many projects go over budget and fail to deliver. In the end, it is up to you to deliver. Allow me to offer some parting advice in the form of the personal development format— *Start, Stop, Continue.*

- *Start* recognizing yourself as *the business*. The prevailing thinking in the data and technology space personifies the idea of "the business" as separate from data and technology. Specifically referring to non-technology roles such as marketing and sales and the personnel who fill them as "the business." If you want to connect what you do to the business, then realize *you are the business*. It is your responsibility to understand what your company does and why. It is part of your role, no matter the job description, to learn, as precisely as you can, about the types of relationships and the value your brands deliver. We cannot progress if there is a separation between data and business. We are the same. YOU ARE THE BUSINESS.

- *Stop* bickering. Please. The data community just loves to wallow in self-absorbed existential pondering. For example, debates rage among us about whether data governance is more significant than data management, or visa versa—or if we should start calling it all "data enablement"—the rest of the enterprise moves on. When we argue on these types of topics, the businesspeople say to themselves, "You see, even they don't agree," and slowly back out of the meeting, leaving us fighting and unfunded.

- *Continue* to do the great work you do. Continue to understand and learn about new techniques and approaches. Continue to listen skeptically to new buzzwords and question their validity and reasons for being. Continue to fight for the power and value of what data can bring to your organization. Continue to update your skills. Continue to learn from what others have done before you.

Your enterprise has a great data story. You just need to find it. Let me know how it goes. Tell me your data story. I want to hear your successes and failures. Remember:

Data management work is never done.

Business is never finished.

Hardware comes and goes.

Software comes and goes.

Data remains.

As everything you do turns to data, this is your opportunity.

Good luck and cheers.

> *Scott Taylor*
> *The Data Whisperer*
> *Black Rock, Connecticut*

Index

Printed in Great Britain
by Amazon

76119014R00112